THE DEVIL'S PLAN

VERSUS

GOD'S MERCY

VERNON GOFF

WESTBOW
PRESS®
A DIVISION OF THOMAS NELSON
& ZONDERVAN

WestBow Press books may be ordered through booksellers or by contacting:

WestBow Press
A Division of Thomas Nelson & Zondervan
1663 Liberty Drive
Bloomington, IN 47403
www.westbowpress.com
844-714-3454

Scripture taken from the King James Version of the Bible.

ISBN: 978-1-6642-0705-9 (sc)
ISBN: 978-1-6642-0704-2 (hc)
ISBN: 978-1-6642-0706-6 (e)

Library of Congress Control Number: 2020918777

Print information available on the last page.

WestBow Press rev. date: 08/19/2022

INTRODUCTION

A SHORT LIFE OF freedom led to years of prison. I could hardly believe the time had come. The work-release building rose up behind me. I had been counting the days—thirty days, twenty-nine, twenty-eight—and now today I was walking out, a small bag in hand, a check in my pocket, and the past now behind me. A future stretched out before me that just a few years earlier I didn't believe could exist. When did it all start? At what point did I make such a life-changing choice? Why did I make such a turn, and where was it I had missed the road to walk straight? My thoughts were whirling as I walked to the waiting car. I had a lot to face, but I knew one thing: the devil was out to destroy, but God had come to seek and save that which had been lost.

CHAPTER 1

MY GREAT-GRANDFATHER WILLIAM Goff left Georgia with his wife after the Civil War. They settled in Punta Gorda, Florida, and started a family. Grandad Jesse Goff grew up and became a commercial fisherman and moved down to the Everglades area in the Ten Thousand Islands to a place called Fakahatchee, meaning *muddy waters*, several miles north of Everglades City. My dad, Vernon, and his brothers quit school after eighth grade to be full-time commercial fishermen with Grandpa. At the time, they were catching fish for a penny a pound. They caught enough fish to pay for a houseboat, which we call *Liters*. The houseboat was built in 1938 for $1,500. Grandad moved the house to Everglades City around 1950, and it is still there today. It was built from Cyprus trees found about seven and a half miles north of Everglades in a little town called Lee Cyprus. The trees were carried to a sawmill in Jerome. At that time, there was a railroad that came down south through Jerome to Lee Cyprus and went down into Everglades City.

My mother's side of the family was Bogges. She was the granddaughter of Charlie Bogges, who moved to Everglades City from an island in the

Ten Thousand Islands in the 1920s. My grandmother married and they moved to Miami, Florida. My mother was born in 1920. She was named Elizabeth, but they called her Betty. Most of my life, she was called sister Betty. Mother spent a lot of time in Everglades to visit her grandparents. My dad and mother married, and I was born in Fort Myers, Florida, in 1942. We lived in a houseboat until it was time for me to start school. Then we moved into a house on the north side of the river in the Everglades across from the rod and gun club. We lived on the river until 1950. That summer of 1950 in June, my little brother Doyle Roger was born. We then moved into a new home across from the Everglades school. My first year of school was in the community church across the river in town.

A new elementary school was being built. In the meantime, we had class in the school's log cabin cafeteria located next to the original high school. Until we moved in 1950, I rowed in a small skiff across the river and walked three-quarters of a mile to school. Everglades, which means *low swamp land*, was a very small but lively fisher town of about five hundred people. Everglades City itself was an island on the innermost of the Ten Thousand Islands, which reached from Marco Island to Shark River. In the late thirties and early forties, Everglades was doing well. Commercial fishing was great, and people came from all over the USA to take fishing trips with one of the many guides.

At one time, there were about thirty guide boats going out of the rod and gun club. The club had a restaurant, lounge, and rooms. A lot of well-known people went to fish and eat at the club. Over the years, some presidents have stayed there, including Truman, Eisenhower, Hoover, and Nixon. Actors such as John Wayne have also visited this popular stop. The city had a bank, grocery store, warehouse, courthouse, jail, rail car, railroad depot, movie house, and some other small stores.

At one time, Everglades had a hospital with a doctor and nurse.

In the late fifties, shrimping became a big asset to the small town. As a young boy still in high school, I worked at the dock of the rod and gun club cleaning the guide boats. I would sell the fish that the fishing parties didn't clean and take home. Since I was still in school, I only had a small boat with a ten-horsepower Johnson. By the time I was out of school, I had my own commercial fishing gear. Most of us boys had cars by the time we were out of school. Some of the boys I ran around with quit school, but my dad insisted that I finish my schooling. I graduated in 1960. By this time, things had started changing in my town. The railroad had stopped running, Naples (a small town just thirty miles north) had begun growing, and Marco Island was being looked at by investors. Then came Hurricane Donna on September 10, 1960. Because our boats were our livelihood, we had to stay with them. Several families with us took our boats up East Creek, a river in Fakahatchee Bay. We tied the boats to the mangroves. As the tide went out and came back in, we adjusted the ropes. When the hurricane passed, the winds died down, so we all took one boat and went to Everglades to see the damage. Everglades was a sight—ten feet of water in the streets, houses halfway under water, and some swept off of their foundations. I had parked our '57 Chevy on the highest part of the ground by the bridge, and only the antenna was sticking out. When we came to the mouth of the creek, we were in Fakahatchee, which, as the name implies, looked like rough, muddy water.

Chokoloskee is a small town a couple miles south of Everglades. The name comes from an old Indian word that means *old home*. The island was settled in 1874. There is a lot of history in and around Chokoloskee. The island is made up of shells from clams, conchs, and oysters. When I was a boy playing on the island, there were tall mounds on the east side of the island. These mounds were made by the Calusa Indians. I could write about the Seminole Indian wars or the old Smallwood's

3

store where the Indians would paddle their canoes to trade for supplies. Or about Ed Watson who was killed by a few men in front of a store that still stands today. I could talk about the school boat that a cousin of mine built to take children who lived on Chokoloskee to Everglades until a road was made sometime in 1956. Of all the interesting things, the one that impressed me the most was the little Church of God standing tall on its stilts. I remember as a small boy going to the Church of God in a small boat after the road was built.

I would go down, and some of the church people would come to pick me up. Mostly I remember riding down in the back of our old fishing truck. Back then, we had what we called a YPE (young people's endeavor), which was a young people's night that we looked forward to. After church, we would have hot dogs or corn dogs with a cold drink. When I was about thirteen years old, I got saved. I remember praying at an old-time altar. Neither my mother nor my dad ever went to church. I don't think my dad ever knew anything about church. My mother's dad and aunt were Baptists, but I don't remember her saying anything about church. But she was never opposed to me going. Mother started going down on young people's night to help the ladies with after-church meals or when they had fish frys on Saturdays. Conviction got ahold of Miss Betty, and she was born again. The old Betty died, and the new one came up fighting for righteousness. I never knew of her giving up or ever letting down. She never yielded to compromise or ever suggested quitting. I was a different story. I backslid and turned from God. The Lord warns about looking back to the days of sin. Luke 9:62 says, "And Jesus said unto him, No man, having put his hand to the plough, and looking back, is fit for the kingdom of God."

I was surely unfit and on my way to a devil's hell at a young age. Don't be deceived; there is only one way to heaven, and it is straight and narrow. In that old-time Church of God, my mother received what we call old-time salvation. It was enough to live by and, at age ninety-three, enough to die by. By the time I was sixteen or seventeen, the boys I ran with and I were no longer strangers to alcohol. We worked hard but partied harder. After Hurricane Donna, things really started to change around Everglades and in my life. The railroad providing both passenger and freight services had ceased in the late 1950s. C. J. Jones Lumber Company burned down in 1956. It was the largest steam-powered mill in the southeastern United States, furnishing lumber at the rate of 100,000 feet per day. The courthouse and jail were moved to Naples, and our bank became a branch bank, which didn't last long. Commercial fishing, guiding, and stone crabbing became our livelihoods, while some restaurants depended on tourists. Now out of school, I was doing full-time commercial fishing and aspiring to be a fishing guide. I first started guiding with my uncle, who had a two-story sixty-five-foot flat-bottom boat for shallow water. We fished along the edge of the gulf and into the inland waters from Everglades to Shark River. We towed our little boats, called skiffs, behind the big boat. We would row the skiffs along the shoreline while the party would cast their lures in hopes for a tarpon or snook. In the early sixties, maybe '62, there was a pretty little girl from Homosassa, Florida. Her dad was a fisherman and a guide who moved his wife and daughter to Everglades. Her name was Betty Ann, but her grandmother always called her Susie, which I picked up on. In 1964, Susie and I were married at Chokoloskee in Uncle Handy's house. He was a preacher and did the honors. We went to Fort Myers for our three-day honeymoon, but because I had a guide trip booked, which I believe was a seven-day Shark River trip, we had to get back quickly.

A few years went by, and my dear mother was still fasting and praying for dad and me. We still refused to go to church with her and still willingly refused the mercies of God. Susie would go and take the children—three wonderful, beautiful children that God had given me. Oh that men would only see how selfish they are—wanting their time and their hobbies, cursing, drinking around the precious children that you brought into the world. Excuses, excuses. Anything but facing the truth. Giving out children examples that affect their own lives as they grow in our footsteps. Showing them all a fake love, a carnal love that is up one minute and down the next. Loving them and their mother one week yet ready to give them up the next. Living by our own selfish feelings rather than by the Word of God. The love of God is the only true love, being unconditional; it looks to the welfare of others. How do our lives affect their lives? Some will say that they would give their life for their children. Maybe so, but you will not give up yourself or your selfish desires for them.

Have you ever stopped and taken the time to question your motives? Have you seriously asked yourself, "Why and for whom do I make my choices?" You must sacrifice self and lead them to Jesus Christ, the only savior of their dear souls. I want my children forever in heaven, not in a devil's hell.

As life moved on and the children got older, we moved out to Ochopee about four or five miles from Everglades. I had grown tired of guiding, and some of my buddies were into stone crabbing and doing well financially, so I thought I would try my hand at that. Stone crabbing begins in winter months and lasts till spring, using baited traps weighed down by concrete and marked with a colored buoy. You break one claw off and leave the other claw. In about a year's time, the claw that was broken off will grow back. So I began building traps, working seven long days a week, and deceiving myself into thinking as long as I was working, the drinking didn't hurt. When I wasn't out pulling traps, I was maintaining the boat. Now many years later, I know that drinking not only hindered my work but also my whole being—my thinking, my actions, my attitude, and my relationship with my wife and our children.

Drinking is one of the deadliest tools Satan has. Give it time, and it will open doors to additional sinful practices, each one piling on top of the other, all leading to a once-promising life being ruined. It will steal your virtue, destroying the morals that you held to for so long, causing you to go right along with the rest of the sinful world. I heard different stories about people making big money in hauling pot, even some of my kin. And it was pretty evident too. Some of the guys who never made any more money than I did were suddenly driving around in new trucks and had new boats. My sidekick—I'll call him Jim—and I had talked about it, and I always said that I didn't want any part of it simply because I felt it was morally wrong (funny how opinions can change). Jim had a different view. We were working hard from daybreak to dark trying to get ahead. This was around forty years ago certainly no GPS, only a compass and our gut feeling. We would have to find our crab line, pull about four hundred traps, then head back home. All told, it generally took us all day, day after day. We were getting ahead financially, but it was one Sunday I'll never forget that would change it once and for all.

We didn't know of any other boats out that day, so we were surprised to see a boat ahead of us. As we moved closer, we could see that the boat was at anchor. We knew who it was long before we reached her side. Everyone knew one another's boats. As I think back and try to gauge the time things started changing, it must have begun in the early seventies, when my dad and older men told me about the government and National Park Department taking over Flamingo south of the Everglades and condemning the houses, financially sinking the man who purchased the town's fish. The older fishermen had said all along the government would move in and take over. I started seeing the change as the National Park Service took over, putting fishermen out of business with restrictions on guiding that made it hard to exist. The government wouldn't grandfather in the old-timers who had made a living all their lives from fishing. Most did not have an education, and it took their livelihood right out from under them. I was in my late twenties, and the park had taken my own home, along with the commercial fishing and airboat riding in the marsh and mangroves, which we once loved and enjoyed. Now no one would enjoy it.

I wonder how much all of that was in my heart as I rode upon that boat that early Sunday morning. How much was all of it in Satan's plan for a young man who was trying to hold the few morals he had left? There was no excuse for my actions; I was just a weak young man taken over by a devil's plan to destroy. Did I really care what other people thought? Was my decision based on my family—my wife and my children? Or was it all about what I wanted? I will never forget the moment we pulled up alongside the boat. The man I knew so well and a cousin of mine were both standing in the back of the boat, and the man I knew well—who was captain of the boat—was shouting to me above the Diesel engine. It was pretty easy to see the bales of pot stacked up high. "Vernon, I know you don't approve of this, but I broke down and need to get this to shore tonight. If you will help me, you won't ever have to pull stone crab traps again."

So there I was. Standing in the pilothouse with three men I knew so well and thought a lot of, all of them looking at me and waiting for my answer. Jim already said this was our chance, and the other two men were in a bad fix, broken down with a load of pot and nowhere to run. "Okay, put the bumpers down and load us up." My boat was smaller than the other, with my pilothouse on the bow and the cockpit open. The open deck was needed for working the traps, loading, and unloading. The open deck was also needed for commercial fishing.

But now, rather than crabs or fish, it was being filled with bales of pot. Loading the five thousand pounds didn't take long. For a long time, I had resisted getting involved in this stuff, instead choosing to work long days earning my money legitimately. But now, put into the situation where I could either help my three lifelong friends or turn my back on them—and possibly be shunned by many other lifelong friends and kin in town—I helped them out. The truth is the lure of money has destroyed many lives. My friend was relieved to have the pot off his broken-down boat and on mine. But it was still early in the day, and we couldn't off-load until after dark, so I had to ride my three friends around all day until we could head to shore. Jim and my cousin didn't seem to mind at all, and they were soon busy trying out the pot themselves. I was glad to see the sun sinking low, about to touch the water. I was still out of sight of land, heading to the shore.

We were to meet some smaller boats about halfway up the small, crooked channel. They would take the pot on and off-load it. We hadn't gone very far when one of the small boats met us. There were three men on the boat. They had flown a plane over the boat that we left anchored and knew someone must have picked them up, and as they pulled up alongside my boat, they knew it was me. I had known those men all my life. They were all older than I was, and one of them was really surprised to see me. He at one time had commercial fished with my dad. He was the best man at my wedding. The hopes of getting the pot off my boat didn't last long as they tied up the smaller boat behind mine and, as they were boarding, started explaining how the law was all over the unload spot. Somehow they must have suspected a load was coming in. So I turned around and headed up the coast, now with six men and a small boat to tow five thousand pounds of pot on an open deck. I had been gone from Everglades now a full day and over half a night. Some days were long, and at times we would get back to the dock after dark. But now my wife and family would be worried. I knew by daylight some of the boats from home would be looking for me, and if they were really concerned, the coast guard would be flying. The park plane flew the coast line often.

We made our way up the shore line about fifteen to twenty miles until we found a place we could hide the pot for another day. We would come back at night with a couple of other small boats. Day was breaking when we got the last of the bales off. Now, with my boat empty, we headed offshore again to pick up the boat we had left anchored. The men in the small boat would hide the last of the pot and then run into town and let our families know we all were all right. We towed the boat into port, a place in the Keys, worn out from all the physical and mental events. Again another day was about to end, so we rested that night, looking forward to the long ride home in the morning.

Some things in our past seem to stay more clear in our minds than others. This event in my life (around forty-five years ago) is so clear. I spent more time going over it than most of the other times I try to recall as writing. Two things stand out to me about this time long ago. One is the choice I made on this one day that more than likely changed my direction in life. I still wonder, *What was it about this choice?* I could have gone home and said, "No more." But something happened. Was it greed? Maybe the excitement? Maybe the blindness of a sinner falling to the lure of Satan, the weakness of the flesh to the ways of the world. We can't serve two masters, for you will love the one and hate the other. I was in certain rebellion against God, while his love for me was holding me from instant judgment. I was fighting my way into hell. Another thing that stands out to me in this picture is the six men with me. I had known these men all my life. I had seen them a few days before and talked with them days after this event. But now as an elder and child of God, looking back, I see things so differently, so clearly, and it saddens me to tears. I see how we were all caught in the same trap, as the years would unfold and time would reveal our lives. I think we were all in a sin-filled world—its lights, the false hope, the lies of comfort money could buy, and the happiness that was always just one step away.

The trip home was good and easy, the welcome refreshing. I look back at how happy I was, how great the future now looked. As I sat home with my wife and children, rehearsing the story, I was enjoying the self-glory, not seeing that self and pride walk a path of destruction. A few days later, the man that I had rescued made good on his promise. I now had more money than I had ever seen. With cash in my hands and my pockets full of money, I could now afford to take a few weeks off to stay home and drink my beer. Little did I know at that time what a horrible pit I had willingly jumped into. A moment's decision would have lifetime consequences.

A sinner can be blind to what sin is and its consequences, or he can know for certain these things but go ahead and act against what is right in the eyes of God. Sure, for a sinner, sin can be pleasant for a season. Satan and our carnal self will see to that. But destruction follows. How foolish we are! We get away with something just once, and we pat ourselves on the back, congratulating ourselves. We begin laying foolproof plans on how to do it bigger and better next time. The Bible has something to say about that: "pride goeth before destruction and a haughty spirit before a fall" (Proverbs 16:18). Drugs, alcohol, pornography, ill-gotten money—these are all lures of the devil, but a person still has a choice to either take Satan's bait or reject it. The alcohol, idle time, and money would soon start the cleaning-out process led by Satan. Without Jesus Christ, humans are never satisfied, always wanting something else. We try to fill that empty spot in our being with the things of the world when nothing but the blood of Jesus will do. Have you ever truly given thought to Mark 8:37? Or what shall a person give in exchange for their soul? The flesh, our body, must die, but the soul will live on forever and ever. The soul is the most valuable thing we will ever have, and we sell it so cheaply.

Drugs, alcohol, money, and cares of this world are temporal. Anything you put before God becomes your god. Mark 8:36 says, "For what shall it profit a man, if he shall gain the whole world and lose his own soul?" I had several boats and plenty of stone crab traps, but my mind wasn't on trapping anymore. I would go out some days and sometimes let someone else just take my boat out for me, but that didn't work out well. Until that time, I didn't know anything about smoking weed or snorting cocaine, and I don't remember it having been in our small community. The boys I ran with had a drinking problem, as did I. It was the only drug we used, and I still believe it is one of the, if not *the* worst of drugs. After I got into the circle, I realized drugs were quite common in other places, especially among the colleges. Among our little fishing village, I knew of a few God-fearing, praying people, but as a whole, morals in our town were naturally high. But we were now becoming open to the drug world. There was a storm coming, and weak people like me didn't realize it and would not see until it was too late. A storm of such darkness had to be led by Satan himself, with all his tricks, all his deceiving tools, going against our families and friends, reaching our children and their children. As of today, we still see the effects of evil.

Looking back, I wonder how things happened so fast. So terrible was the storm that all was lost, with only weak memories in the minds of weak people. Strangers and the government have now come in and taken over, erasing all sights of a once-thriving fishing community. I wonder now at what time or at which point of compromise did God decide to lift his influence and his power from the Church of God down on Chokoloskee Island? My mother warned me. She told me it was happening. No one believed it then, and many won't accept it now. As the power that shines the Gospel light began to dim, the darkness of the world crept in, and oh the price that we all have paid. The old paths are not wanted anymore. The flesh will remove the old landmarks and deceive you into thinking you're fine. In 2 Timothy 4:3, it says, "For the time will come when they will not endure sound doctrine; but after their own lusts shall they heap to themselves teachers having itching ears."

Idle time and a wandering mind are a devil's workshop, and so my mind began to turn. If I could make this kind of money helping in a mishap, what could I make being involved in the off-loading itself? It wasn't long until, through people I knew, I was introduced to the man who was looking for someone to off-load. An off-loader's job was to make arrangements to go offshore, take the pot from a mother ship, bring it to shore, and if needed off-load it to small boats to get it into trucks, vans, cars, RVs or whatever was needed. My part was to get it to them in Miami. They were to sell the pot and supposedly help with the transportation, which didn't turn out too well. Eventually, the off-loaders would supply their own transportation, which turned out well for the outlaws on the off-load side. There was a common agreement among the ones involved that if a truck or van or boat was busted, then you were to turn in the newspaper as evidence of the bust. (Keep this in mind, as later in my testimony, I will talk more about this.)

The new friend and I started planning for our first pot deal. I knew the islands, rivers, creeks, and marshland right up to the highway where I would unload our first load. My friend would deal with the Cuban who dealt with South America (Colombia). I finally got the call (no cell phones, only pay phones and landlines) and went to Miami to meet a friend. Of course, we met over drinks. He said we had a deal of about twenty thousand pounds. The boat would be leaving Colombia in a few days, and when the boat got near, they would give me the coordinates, the place to meet the boat with the pot. I had to arrange for a boat large enough to go meet the mother boat, take the pot from it, and bring it to the shore. And it depended on the weather how close the boats could come into the islands. I would meet them at a chosen spot with smaller boats to bring the load in to off-load.

The first load seemed to go smoothly, as we had taken most of the pot to Miami but had a few bales left. I was at a place of business in Everglades, talking with an older man of the town. He said, "I wish I had a bale of pot to sell. I could get rid of it fast and make me some money." I asked him if he was sure about it. "Oh yes," he said. Well, those few bales I had left weren't but a few minutes from him, so I went and got one, threw it in the back of my pickup, and drove up to the place. I went inside and asked him where he wanted it. He said, "Well, where is it?" I took him to my truck parked outside, and there out in the open sat the sixty-pound bale. It took him a minute to process what he was seeing, but then it came—the cursing, yelling, and calling me crazy. But he ended up with it.

The people I was raised with—all of us—from our youth on, ran free in the Glades. We hunted deer year-round. We caught turtles, killed birds, and caught fish, all of which we ate. My cousin and I would go deer hunting, and our goal was to kill one or maybe two, enough to feed the family and that was all. We, our families and grandparents, all lived off the land.

Some things were against the law, but it wasn't enforced, like deer hunting out of season or night hunting. We knew the game wardens, and they knew we hunted. They would even warn us of the places not to hunt because they were being watched. But then came laws against killing birds, then catching turtles. So my point is we weren't afraid of breaking laws then. But now things have changed, as you get less time for killing a man than a turtle. We didn't kill for trophies or just fun; it was a way of life to eat off the land. We would gator hunt and sell their hide for extra money. A few made a living gator hunting with small boats in the backcountry, hunting the head of rivers and bays. In dry seasons, we would walk or use swamp buggies to get to the marsh and cypress lands.

Late one night, a cousin and I were hunting along a canal at the head of Turner's River. We spotted a small gator (the smaller the gator, the brighter the eyes under a light), maybe two or three feet long. We decided he was big enough, and it was my cousin's turn to dive. One would shoot the gator, and as soon as it was hit, the gator most of the time would roll over and stick up a leg. So if the one diving could get to the gator before it sank, it made things a lot easier. I got the rifle, and my cousin took off his shoes, ready to dive when I fired. But I heard him holler and then saw him kick. Now, my cousin was stout and quick but no match for a ground rattler. It struck him twice. I took my knife out because it was thought then that you should cut the bite, but he said not to. So we took a belt, tied it above the bite and headed to town. It was a long trip, and he was in a lot of pain, but he made it all right.

On my way back from Miami with the last sack of money, everyone was happy and excited. My friend and I patted ourselves on the back for such success. The Cuban was happy, and the Colombians were pleased and ready to do business. As I write this with tears in my eyes, I remember (around forty years ago) standing in my bedroom looking out our window, the children swimming in the rock pit. Others were with my family, beer and whiskey were in the cooler, ribs were on the grill. I was thinking to myself, *I've got it made.* My bed was covered with money—no more worrying about bills being due. But while I was having my party, Satan and his devilish imps were having one as well. For they had, with such ease, lured a young man into their web. So deceived, so prideful, and so selfish. Only now through Jesus

Christ can I see how I was destroying not only myself but also my wife and children.

My dear mother stood in the gap between me and my family and hell itself, pleading for mercy to not let us go. Ecclesiastes 1:18 says, "For in much wisdom is much grief: and he that increaseth knowledge increaseth sorrow." My mother had God-given wisdom, and her eyes were fully open to the curse of Satan and his plan. I, who confessed to love her, was crushing her praying and hopeful heart each day. Thank you, God, for such grace, mercy, love, and long-suffering patience. I keep asking, Why do we hurt the ones who love us the most? The answer must be selfishness. I am ashamed of my past and the hurt and shame I caused so many. It hurts to open the doors of my mind and walk once again down such an ugly path. But my prayer is to help someone to stop, call on reason, and check the path they are now taking—and to let them know that true help comes only from Christ our Lord. Sin has a short-lived pleasure; it's not always fun and games.

I may share a few struggles along the way, but first I want to share the one deal that changed my life and almost claimed it. I had many close calls, but this one dragged on for months—and every man has a breaking point. My Miami friend and I were about ready for another load to import. I was spending more and more time in Miami, drinking and hanging out in bars. It was hard to get anything done with so much drinking, smoking pot, and snorting cocaine.

I have been to meetings where coke was piled in the middle of a table, and they would snort it for hours, sometimes days. They would ask me to smoke or snort to join them, but I knew I had enough problems with alcohol. I didn't need to take on anything else. We finally worked out a deal for thirty thousand pounds. I went back to Everglades to work everything out. We had everything set, and it seemed to go smoothly the first night as we brought ten thousand pounds in and hid the rest in a creek. The next day as we were planning to get the rest in, we got the news. A park ranger was showing a new ranger around and found the pot. They brought it in and stacked it in the ranger station. I don't know why they kept it silent and out of the news, but they did. It wasn't in the paper or on the radio. Maybe they knew it would cause trouble—and boy, it did. I called my Miami friend and told him the load had been busted. Now the Colombians were in Miami, waiting on their money from our Cuban contact, which my friend called the Colombian Mafia, for sure a drug cartel.

A few days later, my friend called me and told me that the Colombians had taken him and the Cuban and were holding them and threatening to kill them. They wanted proof about the missing pot. He asked me if I would meet them somewhere between Miami and Everglades. He said not to bring any guns and that they told him they wouldn't bring any either. I agreed to meet them at what we call Forty Mile Bend, about halfway to Miami at an old restaurant that had been closed for some years. I pulled into the old parking lot, just off Highway 41 and wasn't there long before two cars pulled up, one on each side. They all piled out with my friend and their guns. My friend said, "Vernon, they told me there would be no guns."

The leader of the pack said, "I don't go anywhere without my gun," and pulled up his shirt, and I could see why. If all those scars were bullet holes at one time, I couldn't much blame him. They gathered around me, and the leader started asking me questions. I knew I couldn't get to my shotgun behind my seat, and being the animals that they were, I knew my only chance was to show no fear. I kept my eyes on the leader and told him all I knew about the load. I told him that it didn't get in the news, but if he wanted to send me another load, I would make it up to him. We talked for some time, and then I never will forget what he said and how he said it. He said, "Vernon, I like you, but I must kill you, take something back with me to Mr X, a hand or something to show him." He said it just as calmly as could be, as if we were two friends talking about the weather. After standing there, looking at each other, he finally turned, and they got in their cars with my friend and left me standing there. I don't remember if he even said goodbye. On my way back home that day, I didn't know what to think, but I didn't think it was over. A few days later, my friend called and said they had let him go. He sure thanked me for showing up. Just my showing, he said, had saved him.

Soon after, late one night I got a phone call. It was the Colombian. I don't remember just what he said but I know he sounded drunk or coked up. At times, he said nothing. This went for weeks, always late at night. I began to wonder if one night he and his men might show up at my house. I was at my wit's end. I was afraid for my family. I would holler at my children to get away from the windows in case someone was watching to shoot. I would watch them catch the bus for school. Each morning, I would check my truck for a bomb. If a strange car came to town, we would check them out, with our guns aimed and ready.

Then it happened. One morning, he called, and I finally broke. I don't remember all I told him and don't want to, except I did tell him in choice words that he was a coward for not coming and facing me. I now became somewhat the animal I had called them. I had no fear and was arrogant to him. I was deeper in Satan's pit, becoming more of the man that he wanted me to be. I didn't understand then what had happened, why I never heard from him again. Of course, I realized once I had been saved that it was God's mercy hanging on, his grace following me.

Not long after, a friend and I took four men at gunpoint. We held them a night and all the next day until the money that was owed to me was paid. I took about a year (maybe longer) and did nothing but fish and hunt, mostly in my airboat. Sometimes two or three boats would go and stay at some camp. By now, the national park was taking over the Glades. It wasn't long before they had taken more of the property to the east of me. I had a nice home—three bedrooms and two baths, set on the edge of a rock pit right there in my backyard. I could take my airboat, jump in the pit, and run right into the marsh. I could ride all day in one direction. But the park kept closing in, restricting us more and more.

I was frog hunting when a couple of park rangers stopped me and said we couldn't run where we were anymore, and we had to follow them back to the ramp, which was just down from my house where my friends put their boats in and out. We refused, so they watched us until after dark and left.

I knew it was time for me to leave. The government had been taking more and more land, and sooner or later, they would claim my land. The park said I could stay but that I couldn't leave it to my children when I died. I had bought that property and wanted my children to have it in the future. But it was either sell to the park now or it would be the park's later. The park was also taking over the Ten Thousand Islands from Shark River to West Pass, just north of Everglades. This was a deadly blow to commercial fishing and guiding, as commercial fishing was banned, and tight restrictions were put on guiding.

This itself would be a whole new story, but I'll leave it at this: I know that we must have parks, that continual progress—buildings and land for commercial businesses and private homes—must stop in some places. But even an ignorant fisherman could have made better decisions regarding how to protect the land and restrict some things, rather than some of the decisions that had been made.

Now, as Paul Harvey used to say, the rest of the story.

My wife was from Homosassa (Florida), and we had some friends up there, so we had been visiting them, looking for a house. We bought a nice brick home and a wholesale and retail fish house on the river. We had fish, stone crabs, and shrimp. The place was doing all right, but I was running to south Florida, leaving it to my wife more and more. I was ignorant about my master's business (the devil himself) of destroying me and my family's lives.

In 2 Timothy 2:25, it says, "In meekness instructing those that oppose themselves if God peradventure will give them repentance to the acknowledging of the truth."

There was no recovering myself at this point. I had taken the devil's bait. Sin may be fun for a season. It will play you along and then take your soul into eternal hell. It reminds me of the Marlboro Man. Some of you may be too young to remember the Marlboro Man—the big billboard with a pretty scene of a handsome young man on a fine horse, with a nice cowboy hat, smoking a Marlboro cigarette. But they don't show the back side—years later in a Nashville mall, lying on a cot with oxygen, begging people not to smoke.

I met an old friend who was using airplanes to haul pot and had connections in Jamaica. I went down to Jamaica with him a few times—never having real success making a deal to haul pot. I just had a good time. He had an old cargo plane that we used once. We found a good deal on a Queen Air plane. We bought it but finally left it in the Bahamas. The DEA and law were watching us so closely by now we thought it best to leave it.

My Miami friend got me connected with a plane load in Jamaica. We went down and set things up, and he stayed there to meet the plane—another Queen Air, as it turned out—while another friend and I went to north Florida to meet the load and sell it.

We got to a motel close to the airport where the plane was coming into. The pot was compacted into small packages to fit in the plane better. I don't remember the weight, but the bed of my pickup was loaded to the top. We put a tarp over it and parked it out front of the motel where we could watch it from our room. I thought I had it set to where, when I called, this man would come pick it up. He put us off with some excuse, first one day, then another. There we were in a motel, my pickup parked out front and loaded with pot, and police riding through the parking lot at different times. My friend remembered a car rental place just down the road, so he walked down and rented a car, then came and parked it right alongside my pickup. We got our things together and went to my truck. I climbed into the back and started unloading it to my friend in the car. Our aim was to get enough pot off my truck so that it wasn't so easy to see, especially when we had to stop for a few moments at some red light at an intersection.

Loaded down, we waved goodbye to the cleaning ladies and headed to south Florida. Later on, down in south Miami, I ran into that man who kept putting us off. I sat him down in a chair with my .357 at his head, threatening to kill him. He got his friend on the phone, and they promised me the world. I let him go and never saw or heard from him again. He took me for a lot of money. Thank God for mercy and grace—both for that man going away unharmed and for me not letting my anger cause me to do something horrible. Mercy lasts forever, but grace can suddenly end.

I did not even suspect that I was reaching my end. I had no idea how well the devil's plan was working. Once again, I made a deal with another friend for a small load. He had a boat coming that he wanted to split, which was fine with me. My part was supposed to be about ten thousand pounds, but I don't believe it was that much, maybe eight or nine thousand pounds. The big boat was coming fairly close to shore, so we decided to run our small boats out to unload. It got pretty rough that night, and the boat I had was flat bottomed with a little V in the bow. Jumping the waves made my knees buckle; we hit so hard. By the time we got to the big boat with the pot, the flooring was coming loose, so we couldn't load my boat. We loaded the other boats and headed to shore, where I had a couple of boats waiting to take the pot up a river. These boats had lower sides, were more narrow, and could run in shallow water, which our boats, with twenty-five-foot-high sides and twin 225-horsepower engines weren't suited for. The crew and I got the pot up to the head of the river, close to the highway, and I hid the load in a spot right off the river in a place I had explored for years. I was sure no one could find it. We had a couple of small johnboats to move the pot the last hundred feet, across a shallow marsh to the bridge. The boats fit well under the low bridge.

We waited on the vans to cross in a small bunch of mangroves and palm trees just up from the bridge. Everything went well that night. We had unloaded all we had for the night, the empty johnboats were under the bridge, and we were in our little hiding place, talking over the next night and getting ready to leave. It was probably an hour or two before daylight. We heard a car stop on the bridge. We didn't think much about it for the moment.

We sat there quietly, waiting for the car to leave, when we heard another door open and the sound of a radio—not a car radio. We knew then that it was the law. We stayed quiet, hoping they would just leave, but then one of them spotted one of the boats. We all knew then what we had to do. It was between one and two hundred feet across the open marsh to a string of mangroves where we had a small boat with a small motor on it. I couldn't figure out why they had stopped at the bridge; there was no apparent reason for them to do so. And then I was amazed at how so much law had gathered so fast. (I learned later that the law was looking for someone else to the south of where we were at, and the bridge was the most convenient place to stop and look around. They suspected that this other person was using airboats to bring pot to the road. Not seeing or hearing anything suspicious, they started looking around and discovered our boats.)

By the time we were halfway across the marsh, the spotlights were on, and I think they had a couple of dogs. But we were in the mangroves, and that was like throwing Brer Rabbit into the briar patch; the race was over for them, but we had a ways to go. We were through the mangroves and into the little boat, all four of us, on our way out the river. My big concern was that whatever the DEA was doing, there were a lot of them, and surely they were calling for backup to get someone to come up the river. As far as they knew, it was one way in and one way out. I knew if I could reach where I had hid the pot before, we would be all right. I was sure no one knew the back way out of where we were. We reached the hideout, and I cut the motor off. The man we had left to watch the pot said that he heard a boat, and one time it sounded really close. We made sure the camp was clean, took on our men, and stared out. A short way from the stash, day was breaking, and we could hear a helicopter back toward the road. It was sweeping back and forth from the road to the head of the river, and we knew soon it would be over us. There were a couple of things to consider now. If they couldn't see or hear any more of us, maybe they would think we had gotten all the pot out and had somehow gotten past them. But if they spotted us, the search would increase. And where we were and where we were headed, the boat with now five men would leave a mud trail. So we sunk the boat under the branches of the mangrove and put the motor in the mangrove. The Everglades aren't for the weak or sissies. While I was taking the motor off, I sank into the mud up to my waist, and I lost my boots.

We had just gotten fixed and under the trees when the police flew close, and the next pass they made, we could clearly see the men inside the helicopter. A couple of men I was with were careless and had very little to no value for life. I looked over at one point and noticed one had his gun trained on the helicopter. I shouted at him to put the gun down and not dare think about shooting. He obeyed but begrudgingly. I knew we were in enough trouble and didn't need anymore. As the helicopter passed, we moved farther back until we couldn't see them. Time passed, and it wasn't until late that evening that we heard them again. We had been up all the night before, and now as dark came, we tried to rest awhile.

Soon, wet, muddy, with no water or food, we were on our way before the day fully broke. Late that evening, we came to a big bay, and I knew from there it was probably another mile. The men were so tired that I had them stay put and I took one man with me for that last mile. To stay out of the mangrove roots, we walked the shoreline around to the mouth of Everglade River. Night had fallen before we got to the river, and now we had to swim. The current was strong, and I was weak. My friend made it across to where he could touch the bottom. I had a little ways to go, but I could hardly lift my arms to cut water. Even now, I remember my friend hollering to me, "You should be able to touch the bottom," and when I would stop and try to touch the bottom, my head would go under, and I could hardly make it back up. I was at my end when finally I felt the bottom. The devil's plan had almost come to its end. I'm sure he thought he had me. But mercy had once again stepped in, even though I was a wicked sinner and doing the devil's work.

I wonder how many people come close to death or an accident and never think of God, the ruler of the universe. As a teenager, at seventeen or eighteen years old, I came home one morning, having been out all night drinking. My mother met me at the door, tears in her eyes. She said, "Son, what happened? You were almost killed." How did she know a gang member had pulled a pistol on me and a police car just happened to pass by and saw it? They pulled in to stop the quarrel. She had been praying all night with a burden, and I never thanked her or God. The bad part is I can't make it up. But now I can thank my God every day of my life for his great love, grace, and mercy.

We had one more canal to swim, and then we made our way to a friend's house and got him to take us in his boat to pick up the other men. Another night had almost passed by the time all of us made it home. Four or five days had passed since the morning we had to run from the law. Now the one who gave my friend the pot wanted some answers. He had explained to them what happened, but now the question was, Did the law find the pot? Or could it still be saved? I knew the pressure would be heavy upon him, so I told my friend to give me two days to check things out, and I would go in and see if it was still there. One of the men who had been with us from the start joined me, and we got a few things together. He was more than ready to go with me. Needless to say, he had been by my side in many adventures, and I could depend upon him in any situation.

The morning we were going to leave, my friend told me that his contact insisted that one of their men go with us. We weren't happy with that at all. He was a young fellow, and we could tell he felt his importance. He was all about making sure things went right. It took a while winding through small creeks and bays. We began getting closer, and the creek was getting smaller. At times, we had to hold the mangrove limbs over the boat. As we got closer to where the pot was hidden, I shut the motor off to listen. Our passenger wanted to know why we had stopped and told us to go ahead. Around the second time this happened, I was getting upset, and I knew my friend wanted to throw him out of the boat. I was trying to be careful, and I knew the pot was close, so I stopped again. Our passenger said, "What's wrong with you guys? You afraid?"

By then, I had had enough of him, and I knew what my friend was thinking, so I told him, "Look, the pot is up that creek a ways, and when it ends, there is a little bay. Turn to your left, and it should be right there. Now you're so brave and anxious, get overboard and start swimming."

The water wasn't deep, maybe waist deep, but really muddy. I was surprised, but he eased over the side. I don't know if he sort of knew he didn't have much choice or what. We sat there for a little while, talking, when we heard him scream. Then he started yelling for help, for us to come and get him. We knew then that our being quiet was all in vain. Anyone within half a mile would have known that we were there. We started the motor and went to him, and when we got there, we didn't have to help him into the boat. All thoughts of leaving him there were gone after seeing his change in behavior. He got into the boat, sat down, looked at the bottom, and never said another word. I still don't know what happened to put him in such a state. Sometimes we might see a snake, or when going up a small creek, at times fish will hit you or even jump around you. The water was still salty for lack of rain, so the chance of a gator wasn't likely. Even after my friend and I got into the water and left him to go see about the pot, he never moved. It was all there, safe and sound, so we headed back to Everglades to make arrangements to bring it out.

When we got to the dock, our friend jumped out and started walking, still not talking to us. We got the pot the next night, to the north of where we were. A few days later, my friend asked me what had happened with our passenger. He told me that he had walked to the highway and had hitchhiked to Miami. He told them that those men down in the Everglades were crazy and he would never go back there again.

The devil was trying to destroy me, just as he is you and every one of God's creatures. But one thing we must always remember is we have free will, and it is we who make the choices. Each day, we choose our destiny. The devil can influence us. He has a lot of tricks, but we make the choice. Is it not a wonder that the most important thing that we own—our soul—we treat so carelessly? Heaven or hell eternally, with God's Word to direct us, and we don't take the time to read it. It's not as if we are thrown out by ourselves to be destroyed by the devil. God keeps the rightful balance. He is always near with open arms. Nature itself reveals God. The Holy Ghost is always revealing Jesus. The Word tells of the suffering, shame, death, burial, and resurrection of our Lord and savior, Jesus Christ.

Watson's house on Chatham Bend

My Father, Vernon Goff SR.

CHAPTER 2

THE PRESSURE WAS on.

I had moved to Cape Coral, north of Ft. Myers (Florida). The law was closing in, watching wherever I went. I had a fifty-channel scanner on my truck, plus a lot of friends listening. I was heading to the Keys, working on a small deal from the Bahamas. While on my way, I stopped in the Everglades. A friend stopped me and said I had better be careful, whatever I was doing, because the DEA was following me and the other car I had heading down. I got in touch with the other car, told them to stay at Homestead and load the trunk with potatoes, and I'd meet them in Ft. Myers. On my way back, I stopped at a marina, not far from where I had unloaded the pot a couple of times. I wasn't in the bar long before several agents came in. After years now, I could spot an agent pretty quickly. I would drink a while, then go to the pay phone and call a friend who was on the scanner. He would tell me what they were saying, and I won't repeat the number of them that he told me were on my case, thinking I was at the marina waiting for a load, but it was a lot of them.

The next day, I got a motel room and went into town. I wasn't gone too long and then returned to the room. The phone rang. It was a friend, a different one from the last. I asked him how he knew where I was. He laughed and said it was all over the scanner, that the DEA had just left my room. I checked out and went to Cape Coral to my house. Later on, maybe a week or so, I went to one of my favorite places to hang out. It was a lounge on the river with a swimming pool and a three- or four-story hotel. The woman I was with was lying out by the pool, and after some time, I walked out to talk to her. She said to me, "Don't look up now, but there are men on the roof watching us with glasses." I told her to wait there about five minutes, then to go to the room and get everything together. I would meet her there. We took our things, jumped in my truck, and turned the scanner on. As I left the parking lot, they said, "He's turning (onto some street)," but then I turned the other way and went in and out of different places until I knew I had lost them. I pulled into a car lot, bought a car, loaded our things and the scanner, and left town for a while. I knew if they had anything on me, they would have arrested me, so I was just having fun with them at the time. But I'm sure it cost me later, because they were mad.

A week or so later, as soon as I pulled into town, the scanner said, "VG from CC is back in town." I went and had a tag made for the front of the car that read "VG from CC." Seemed funny at the time, but my arrogance, thinking I had everything under control, was soon going to have its payday. Things seemed to quiet down after I had been in town a while. There were several reasons for this, I believe. One, maybe the law (which consists of the DEA, county sheriffs, federal marshals, and sometimes the Coast Guard) knew I was aware of their constant watch. Another thing was they had busted a van load with pot, and the person caught was cooperating with them. One person, one witness, can lead to the arrest of many. Lots of people, men and women, were willing to do the crime, but there were always a few not willing to do the time. A few nights in jail, and they were ready to make a deal—anything from no time to less time to being an informer or just witnessing against others. Another thing that made it look as though they had lost interest in me was (which I learned sometime later) that they were trying to set me up. They had busted a shrimper and made a deal with him to use him and his boat to set up as a pot hauler, and I was a target. I had heard of agents getting in with different jobs and crews, working with them and then busting the whole crew.

I had an experience with a setup once. The agent wasn't in the off-load crew but with the Cubans who set up the deal in Colombia. They sent a boat all the way there and back, and somehow they got an undercover agent in the crew. I don't know if the agent was going to try and go to shore with the off-load crew or not. This wasn't my deal, and I didn't know the men who arranged the load. I knew the off-load crew and was to be inland to help them. The friend who knew them called me at the last minute and asked if I would take the four Cubans to meet the shrimp boat with the load. They wanted to be there off-loading from the shrimp boat to the smaller boats. I told him I would and made arrangements to meet them in Naples, where I took them to a boat I had gotten ready. I took a friend with me that I trusted. Things can go bad in many ways in this business.

It was already getting late by the time we broke out into the Gulf in open waters. We had to run to the north an hour or so in pretty rough water. We didn't have GPS to tell the exact spot, how long to get there, and how fast we were running—just a compass, coordinates, and maybe a depth recorder. (When I first started stone crabbing, all we had was a compass and a string with a weight for a depth recorder.) Night was on us, the stars were out, and we still had a mile or two to reach our destination when we spotted the boat. I pulled alongside as close as I could, with it being rough. The Cubans verified that it was the boat we were looking for. The boat was south of where it was supposed to be, so the Cubans told them to follow us to connect with the off-load boats. Now I was in a Scarab (speed boat) with four Cubans and a friend, leading a shrimp boat with thirty thousand pounds of pot in water that I was not familiar with, looking for an offloading crew. I had no idea anything was wrong. I found out later that the offload crew and the ones on shore had detected that the law knew a load was coming, and they all dismissed any action. There wasn't any way to get in touch with me to warn me. A couple of men told me later that after everything was shut down, they listened on the police scanner as the law proceeded to bust the shrimp boat.

I calculated I was near the spot to meet the off-load boats. As we were looking for any sign of a boat, we saw a light just a short way in the direction we were heading. As we were looking, I told my friend that things didn't add up. One, there should not have been any lights. Two, the light we saw was too high off the water. I turned the boat directly into the sea and gave full throttle. We were up running when lights came on. Blue lights, spotlights, running lights. There was a helicopter to our left, and from somewhere came a fast-running boat about our size. Police have informers—outlaws—and many of the houses have police scanners. I asked a law officer who I knew well why they said things that we could detect, and he said when things got close to happening, there was always someone who couldn't help themselves and had to say something. The boat I had was narrow in the bow and cut the waves well. I noticed the boat behind us wasn't cutting the waves, and each wave slowed it some, so I kept running into the waves, not knowing where I was at this point, except I was heading into shore. There was a lot of fire in the water (we homefolk call it fire, but it's phosphorus, something found in matches), and I was afraid the helicopter could see me a long way off, busting through the waves, looking like a blaze each time. It looked like we had lost the boat behind us. I turned toward the south, riding sideways to the wave for a time and then turning back off shore. I slowed to almost an idle.

My friend and I were trying to decide what to do. I didn't know the area we were in. I didn't know if we had enough fuel to go back south or how many more boats the law had. And in any position, my friend and I being caught with four Cubans we didn't know would not be good. The four men with us wanted to go to shore. I told them I didn't know the area, and for sure, any dock in the inlet would have the law. But they insisted on going to shore. I was ready to take them to shore and surely didn't want to spend the rest of the night with them, dodging the law. So we headed to shore.

I followed the beach down a little ways, and seeing an inlet, I started in. It turned out that there was a small channel between two beaches, and through the gap, it opened into a long, narrow bay. The beach side was lined with mangroves, with a mangrove island in the bay. Just inside the gap, the channel made a turn. On the left was a sand bank, and on the right was a mangrove island. Across the bay was a small marina with a boat ramp. I was sure that was where the law was working out of. I ran the boat on the sandbar, and it keeled over to one side. On the way in, we made sure anything that we didn't need or that would lead to us was thrown overboard. The boat had hardly stopped when the four men were over the side and headed down the sandbar, with about a foot of water on the bar. My friend and I took the other direction. We hadn't gone but a few yards when I turned and went back to the boat. He asked what I was doing, and I said that I had a jug of water I had brought, just in case. I wasn't planning to hide out in the salty mangroves without fresh water again. We waded out to the small channel and swam across to one of the islands, then worked our way down the bay until we

33

thought it was safe. It wasn't long before we heard the boats and saw the spotlights searching. We knew they wouldn't find us as long as we stayed in the mangroves in the water, but what about after daylight? We sure didn't want to stay in the mangrove all day and another night.

As daylight was breaking, we were making our way out toward the middle of the bay to a small mangrove island with a spot of sand on one side. We made our way around to the east side of the island and set up in the mangrove to rest and decide what to do next. We weren't there long after daybreak when we saw a small boat leaving the channel that came by the island and heading our way. We watched as the older man anchored his boat and proceeded to get his fishing gear ready. All set, he baited the hook and cast the bait right to our feet. I thought it was now or never. We didn't want to scare him, but he would see us anyhow, so we waved and started out to him. "Sir, we are sorry to mess your fishing up, but we were on the island last night, and sometime during the night, our canoes went adrift." We asked him if he would take us across the bay to the shoreline and drop us off. He was really nice and more than glad to help us out. We climbed in the little boat, maybe sixteen feet, and pulled the anchor, and he headed down the channel. We said, "Sir, just take us straight across the bay to the shoreline."

"Oh no," he said. "I'll take you right back to the dock at the marina. I don't mind at all."

"But, sir, that's out of your way. Just drop us off anywhere across the bay." He was determined to take us back to the marina, so we just sat down and tried to act like we really appreciated his kindness, knowing that the DEA and probably most of the law was there, looking for smugglers.

He pulled up to the dock out front of the marina, and as we got out, he said he wished us luck. We were thinking we sure needed it. We wished him a good day fishing and went up to the outside counter and bought a couple of drinks with wet money, then went and sat down at a picnic table. We watched them get the helicopter ready for another ride and the law at the boat ramp. I had walked over to a pay phone and called a friend of mine to come get us. An hour or so later, our ride came. We got into the car, and another ordeal was over. I never heard anything about the four men again.

Now, back to me being set up by the law. The shrimper they used was said to be from North Carolina, another one that was riding high until he got caught. He turned to the law to help catch someone else in order to either lower his time to be spent in prison or to have the charges dropped against him. About the time they were trying to trap me, the law caught a man driving a van with pot. His turning on his own people led to the bust in Everglades City. The law had gotten this shrimper with his boat in with someone—a fisherman from Tarpon Springs. Now another friend of mine and I were looking for a boat to go to Colombia. So, I met with him and told him I might be interested but not for sure. I had met this man before with a friend of mine. It turned out he was the one the law had really set up. He wanted to know if I wanted to meet with this shrimper from North Carolina and see his boat. I told him no. At the time, I didn't know if we were going to even need the boat. I gave the man $10,000 to keep the boat around for two weeks, just in case.

A few days later, he called me and wanted to know if I would talk to the shrimper on the phone. By now, I knew something wasn't right. Why keep pushing me to meet someone I didn't know? I told him I wasn't talking to anybody and we wouldn't need the boat anyhow. I didn't meet him or talk to him any more after that, and the friend who had introduced me said he didn't hear from him either. A good while went by, maybe a year, and I guess somehow the law worked with him, and when they revealed themselves to him, they scared him into talking. A newspaper said that a Tarpon Springs fisherman served as a confidential informant for the sheriff's department, which also provided the crew for the smuggler's boat. I'm not sure if the paper meant that the informant provided the crew for the smuggler's boat or the law. Either way, they lured him into enough willingness to make big money that he got himself a big conspiracy charge. The *Tampa Bay Times* says it was a yearlong undercover drug operation from 1984. Then the *Tampa Tribune* for Wednesday, February 13, 1985, ran an article on two men being arrested on marijuana charges. "Police say 2 men have been arrested and charged with plotting to traffic marijuana on alleged drug activities worth an estimated $250 million in street sales. Arrested were Edward Clark of Port St. Joe and Vernon Goff of Cape Coral. Both were charged with conspiracy to traffic in excess of 10,000 pounds of marijuana." The article also states that they were placed under a $500,000 bond each. My arrest was not a real surprise. I had an attorney in Tampa who was watching for a warrant for my arrest. The state law was working with the feds, and the feds dropped the case (for a lack of evidence), and the state (Florida) took it up. So I was aware of the state working up a case. I just didn't see how they could prove anything, not even being caught with anything.

I had just gotten back to Ft. Myers to the place where I was staying. It must have been around two in the afternoon. I wasn't there very long when the phone rang. It was my attorney's secretary, who I had come to know very well. She said, "Vernon, they have a warrant for your arrest." I told her thanks, then hung up and told the girl that was with me that I had to leave quickly and I'd get in touch with her later.

Then a loud knock on the door came with a voice: "Police." I turned to go out the back when the girl with me said that they were out back too. So, I went to the door and told them I was going to open the door and that I didn't have a gun. I had nothing against the DEA agents or the police. But I know they are human, and sometimes the name *drug dealer* makes some of them nervous. They handcuffed me, put chains on my feet, and walked me out to their car. One of them had both hands on his gun and was shaking. I told him to relax and to put the gun down because I wasn't going to do anything. They took me to the county jail and a couple days later flew me into St. Petersburg. We had hardly gotten off the runway in the little single-engine plane when the agent next to me got his notebook out and started asking me questions. I told him that he might as well put the notebook away, as I wasn't going to say anything. If he had any questions, he needed to ask my lawyer. This was all new to me. I had never been arrested, never spent the night in jail, never been booked. My pride and arrogance got me through pretty well.

Being so selfish, so self-centered, I couldn't see all the hurt that I was causing the ones I claimed to love so much. As the news reached my family, my children … it hurts me even now to think of the tears, the feeling of fear and uncertainty that must have gripped them. Their world was turned upside down, and I—so deceived, so tough—wouldn't let anyone see me cry. Fact was I couldn't cry. My conscience had become seared, and my heart had become dangerously hard. The devil had a plan for me, just as he has a plan for you. The plan is the same that he revealed in the Garden of Eden—to deceive, divide, and destroy. The devil wants you to join him in that lake of fire and brimstone, suffering torments for all eternity.

It wasn't long until I was back on the road again, out on bail, not too concerned about the charge. My attorney at first seemed to think I had a good chance of beating the case. My faith was in money and in man—a vain, useless faith. I had known the lawyer long before my arrest. My brother-in-law was on probation and charged with shooting a gun in city limits. The attorney told me it would cost $5,000, and just a few days before trial, he said it would take another $5,000. But my brother-in-law walked out of court without probation or a fine. I was pretty confident that my attorney knew the right people. As time drew closer to the trial date, my attorney didn't sound very sure. I checked with him for any changes, but his whole outlook on things wasn't encouraging at all. He told me they had changed judges; one he didn't know would be hearing my case. A short time after that, I went by his office, and he had me go into his private office and closed the door. He said, "Vernon, it doesn't look good for you. They are out to get you." He told me that if I would leave for a while and give the case time, we could probably beat it. I asked him how long it would take, suggesting perhaps a year or two, and he said yes. I could go on, tell you about my anger and things I found out about my attorney and my trial. But I don't want to seem to be trying to exempt myself from my wrongdoings. I'll just say I wasn't caught in the act and knew I had been set up.

I went back to Ft. Myers and in a few days went to see my mother and dad. They were living at Chokoloskee Island. I will never forget sitting in the living room, telling them all I knew about my case and how I would more than likely be convicted. I was facing a minimum of fifteen years. I told them some of my plans to leave the country for a few years. Then something happened that I had never seen in my lifetime. My strong, tough daddy, whom I had never told that I loved him, broke down and cried like a child. My mother just hung her gray-haired head with tears in her eyes. In her God-given wisdom, she knew that if I left the country, it would most likely be my end. After a time of silence, just looking at one another, I assured them that I would stay and take my chance at the trial.

Thinking back on my life, how things came about, I remember when my life took a terrible turn. I wrote earlier that after the back and forth with the Colombians, something happened within me. The morals

I had been raised with—the "yes, sir, no sir"—no more mattered to me. Respecting others no longer had any value. The very ones I talked about, the Colombians, and how the lives of others meant so little to them—they became little to me.

As I drove away from my mother and dad, back to Ft. Myers, I was ready to face the trial. Once again, something happened to me. I wasn't aware of the change then, but now I realize that God's mercy had stepped into my life. Over the next few weeks, I can't say I wasn't aware of my drinking problem, but there is a big difference in being aware and finally admitting, "Yes, I am an alcoholic." It ruled my life. In fact, it hurt not only me but also those around me I loved so much. I am still amazed today how God keeps on with a sinner—his great love, his long-suffering patience, even while we rebel each day, rejecting him, mocking him, treading on the blood of Jesus, his only begotten Son.

Ephesians 2:4: "But God, who is rich in mercy, for his great love wherewith he loved us." Ephesians 2:5: "Even when we were dead in sins, hath quickened us together with Christ, (by grace ye are saved)."

God has given us, his creatures, a free will. We ourselves choose right from wrong. He has given us a conscience to guide us. God will not violate his own law. He will not override our free will to choose. He keeps all things in order, making our choices fair and balanced. The devil has his plan to destroy each of us, leading us into the same hell that he is headed for. God has a plan for us too, which is life eternal, living in the real world, heaven. You ever wonder why one would choose hell over heaven? We sure are full of excuses. The flesh will fight to survive. The flesh will even make a deal with you. Just don't go too far or get too serious. The flesh loves religion, as long as it involves works and not true salvation, a salvation that crucifies the flesh and keeps it in subjection.

Galatians 5:24: "And they that are Christ's have crucified the flesh with the affections and lusts."

The time for my trial had come. The girlfriend I had been with for the last few years went with me to St. Pete. My mother and dad insisted on going too, so I got a motel close by the courthouse. It was thought that the trial could last as long as two weeks. I believe it was the second day that the jury went in to determine my case. We left for lunch and were to be back at a given time. Before we started back, I told my mother and dad that if I was convicted, they would handcuff me right then, and I would get in touch with them as soon as possible. I gave my girlfriend my watch, wallet, and ring and went back to court. It didn't take long before the jury came back with a charge of guilty. Some of my family was there. My son told me later that when the judge said twenty-five years, they handcuffed my hands behind my back, and I just turned around to them and smiled, as if to say, "I'll see you later."

Proverbs 18:12: "Before destruction the heart of man is haughty, and before honour is humility."

After the trial and sentencing, I was in the court jail for several months, then sent to Lake Butler. If you are given any time over a year sentence, you are sent to a state prison. Anything less than a year is spent in the county jail. Lake Butler is where they process you. Lake Butler is in North Florida, south of Lake City. All prisoners are sent there and then to a prison according to the crime—minimum security or maximum security and supposedly to a prison closest to your home. I understand that now there is another place like Lake Butler in Miami. I was at Lake Butler for seven months, with still no contact with my family. Finally, after medical exams and them seeing how well I knew my ABCs, I was sent to Polk Correctional—a maximum security prison located around Lakeland, Florida. I was sent to maximum security with the razor wire and gun trucks, I think for several reasons. My crime was not violent, but the twenty-five-year sentence in prison was a life sentence, and they would be able to make a deal with me after being locked up for a while. They came to me twice, hoping I would talk, as I knew a lot of people.

I got to Polk Correctional on the Bluebird Express. They led us into a cage and took the cords and leg chains off and then took us into the prison yard. There was a group of cons waiting to meet us at the gate. I knew not to talk to anyone and not to accept anything from them. In the prison system, there is a hierarchy, and they don't give without an alternate motive.

I got settled into one of the dorms. The dorms were open with a closed-in ground room, mostly glass, where they could watch all things at all times. The showers and toilets were all open right across from the guards. There were maybe seventy cots with just enough room to walk between them and one metal drawer under each cot. There was one phone in the dorm, always with a long line, and when you did get through, it was so loud you could hardly hear. But I got through to my mother and got set up for money in my account in the prison for the canteen. We also discussed how she could make arrangements for visiting. Now I think back on how I was in anger, going through all the hoops in the prison. All about me. I don't remember once thinking about my dear mother for months. I wasn't in touch and didn't care or think of the fact that she wouldn't even leave the house, for fear of missing my call. My dad would take a fishing trip all day with a party, get in at the dock, clean fish for them, then rush home to see if I had called yet. Now they were excited to hear from me and to know who to contact to set up a visiting time. I was sure ready to see someone that I knew loved me and I trusted with my all.

The prison was a big place. I don't remember how many acres the whole complex was, but I started walking around to get more familiar with the place. I spent a great deal of time walking around a track. Exercise was big in prison. An old inmate I got to know told me one time, "Vernon, you see all the men walking and running around the track? They weren't arrested; they were rescued. Outside, they would be drinking and taking drugs and would not eat. Now they get three meals, get taken care of, and are getting ready for the streets again."

One day I was at the place to receive mail, and someone called my name. I was surprised that anyone knew me. I believe there were around seventy men in there. It took a few moments to recognize who this man was. I probably hadn't seen him since he was in his teens. He was in for murder, and I believe, at the time, he said he had been in for fourteen years. He was one of the (we might say leaders). All knew him. We talked a while, and he explained a few dos and don'ts. He said I needed to get out of the dorms and into the special units. These units were two-story buildings with two-man rooms, about eight by ten feet, with a double bunk, sink, and toilet. It was much more private. It took a while to be able to get into one of those units. You had to get on a list and have good behavior, which took a long time. No one wanted to lose their spot and be put back into the overcrowded dorms. Well, prison has politics, and I knew the top in command. I was soon in a room on the second floor, invited to my first prison wine party.

Before I move on from the dorm, I want to mention Mr. Berry. The dorms were loud, and there was always a long line to use the phone. There weren't as many fights as there was shouting. I wasn't long off the streets, still very prideful and arrogant and not much for shouting. Mr. Berry kept me out of a lot of trouble. He was a big man, well over six feet and maybe 220 pounds. He was one of the first men I met. He had lived close to where I was in Homosassa Springs. He hung out at the same restaurant where I spent a lot of time. There was a little motel at the place, and he had caught his wife with another man in one of the hotel rooms. He shot them both with a rifle. Mr. Berry would see me get fighting mad in the dorm and call me to the side more than once to talk me out of doing something foolish. It's not uncommon for someone to go to prison for a year or two and end up serving many years. There was a lot of shouting at one another, name-calling, and threatening. It was as if the loudest won. They seemed to want attention. I wasn't for shouting. The first punch had the advantage. Mr. Berry's sentence wasn't very long, considering the crime. I don't remember the time he started with, but at the time I knew him, he had five years. The prison system was crowded, and they were giving out extra gain time in bunches. Gain time was given to a prisoner according to good behavior and if you worked at some position in the system. I worked in electrical maintenance and gained twenty extra days a month. So serving a fifteen-year sentence, you would really end up serving only around six years. I never received my extra gain time, and I guess that's because of my sentence—conspiracy to import marijuana. I never understood that. Mr. Berry and most others would sometimes get twenty days up to 120 days of extra gain time. I'm sure some of this has changed over time. So, Mr. Berry's custody was lowered, and they removed him from maximum security to another prison. I didn't see or hear from him for a long time. One day, Mr. Berry showed up again, which I will talk about later on.

Now back to moving from the crowded dorms. I had been in prison long enough to know my time was running out. I would either get in some trouble or try to leave. Most inmates seemed as though they would just as soon be there as at home, and they seemed to know one other and had a good time.

I was really relieved when they called my number to report to the office to tell me to get my things together. I was moving to the two-man dorms. My new friend showed me the room. It was upstairs, across the hall from him. He introduced me to my new roommate, who he was friends with. My new roommate was a young man who was polite and quiet. He had been in prison for about five or six years, and we always got along. He never talked about his past, and I never asked. I was told he was in for double murder, but if you had just met him on the street, you would never have known. I met his parents later on in the visiting park and thought highly of them as well. These two-man rooms were quiet compared to the big dorm, and these guys had it together for the situation and looked out for one another, so the stealing was not bad. I felt as though I could hold on a little longer, and I kept to myself as much as possible, but seeing the same men each day, I got to know some of them.

One man was a plumber before he arrived and must have been good at his profession because he kept the whole prison compound up. The plumber was a quiet man and always busy. He had been in prison I think for twelve or thirteen years at that time. He was in for murder, just as many of the men there, having committed the crime in a moment of anger. Moments of temper, overcome with anger, destroys lives. Most of the men I got to know didn't talk very much, if at all, about their crimes. Some, I believe, were ashamed, and for some, it was hurtful.

Then there was Lester, a man of small stature, who always seemed happy and easygoing and never got into any trouble. He didn't mind telling his story, how he and another man got into an argument at a bar and how he took his sawed-off shotgun, pointed to the man's head, and blew it off. Just before I went to work release, Lester was working at the prison water plant, just outside the prison. He had at that time served about fourteen years. In a prison of about nine hundred men, there was any sort of spirit one can imagine. I marvel at how God could take one as wicked of a person as I was in that place and break me down (I had to be broken), then raise me up from a babe in Christ right in the devil's backyard. It shows that if you totally yield to God, God will give you the power to serve. Our part is to continually stay close to him through daily prayer, fasting, and reading the Word of God. Idolatry, witchcraft, uncleanliness, lust, lying, murder, jealousy, and deceiving are just some of the spirits that you find in prison. They are the same spirits that you find outside the walls; the only difference is that in prison you can't get away. I talk about this because I don't think very many people realize the spirits we are in daily contact with. And I see very little discernment among those who claim to follow Christ. We look at people, the flesh and blood that is standing before our eyes, rather than the soul and spirit that is leading them.

One of the main points of the Bible is in Ephesians 6:12: "For we wrestle not against flesh and blood, but against principalities, against powers, against the rulers of the darkness of this world, against spiritual wickedness in high places." Whatever God is for, Satan is against. And two of Satan's basic weapons are deception and confusion. Did he not use these against Eve in the Garden? Satan will always attack God's Word—the Bible—and either deceive people into thinking that they can break God's Word and there will be no consequences, or he will confuse people by causing them to hold onto a false interpretation of the truth, such as by suggesting that something applied only to the Old Testament but doesn't apply to today. This happens when the flesh is not totally crucified. God made man and then a woman for a helpmeet. God said in Deuteronomy 22:5, "The woman shall not wear that which pertaineth unto a man, neither shall a man put on a woman's garment: for all that do so are abomination unto the Lord thy God." Satan will disrupt the identity between man and woman, which God had ordained to be totally separate in looks. A man is to look manly, and a woman is to look feminine. They are to hold their God-given place.

Leviticus 20:13 says, "If a man also lie with mankind, as he lieth with a woman, both of them committed an abomination; they shall surely be put to death; their blood shall be upon them." Satan is trying to get people to believe that it is all right to change the gender that God gave them while in the womb. Until prison, I didn't know how the homosexuals were coming out of the woodwork, so to speak. It was sickening to see a man put on tight shorts with makeup, strolling around and acting like a woman, causing trouble where he/she went. One morning, I heard a commotion in the hall a couple of doors down. Looking out, I first thought it was just another fight. But soon I realized that one man had stabbed another man as he came out from the showers. He stabbed him a couple of times, but I believe the first blow killed him. He was dead when he hit the floor. The man had hidden a can of paint thinner and was going to use that to pour on his lover and set him afire after he had stabbed him. Some of the inmates, though, stopped that. What was it all about? Homosexuals fighting over one of their lovers. A man jealous over another man. Nothing but lustful spirits in full swing. We have gotten so used to them now that they seem to most people just natural. It is an abomination to God. Leviticus 18:22 says, "Thou shalt not lie with mankind, as with womankind; it is an abomination."

Take God out of our homes, and what happens? Take God out of our country and our schools? Without God, we will fail.

I was in maximum security with many of these men who had already served five or ten or fifteen years. I want you to keep in mind that I hadn't been in prison yet a year. I still had connections on the outside but now also knew the ropes on the inside. It wasn't long before my roommate, my friend, and I had a business going—a hidden place with pot and money. A lot of weed is smoked in prison. (I didn't smoke it. I was an alcoholic.) I had been in the county jail but now was in prison, and I had not had a drink in over a month. I had no withdrawals and no DTs, but I was still an alcoholic. Our group had (they bragged) the best homemade wine. They saved all the fruit they could get and had connections with the kitchen for sugar. We'd get plastic milk jugs and hide them until we were ready—sometimes in the ceiling or maybe in the yard under some plant. Do you get the picture of a man driven by the devil on the broad road to hell? Blinded, deceived, not even seeing the daily misery of sin, let alone the future damnation. Continually looking for peace and love when it was always at hand. In fact, a nail-scarred hand was reaching down to deliver at any time. I was too busy looking around for a place to escape. Oh that I would have only looked up, reached up to the one reaching down. But grace was following me, mercy keeping me.

I was at my wit's end. As the Bible says in Psalm 107:27, "They reel to and fro, and stagger like a drunken man, and are at their wits end." I was in my forties with a twenty-five-year sentence hanging over my head. The devil had me convinced my life was over. Dragging through the days, I woke up each morning depressed. I was a captive of the devil, not able to escape. I had been in prison for over a year. Even at best, I couldn't make it five or six more years. In 2 Timothy 2:26, it says, "And that they may recover themselves out of the snare of the devil, who are taken captive by him at his will."

The group of men I was around each day didn't talk about religion, except to make fun of those who professed religion. Prison is the same as the world; the company you keep is really choosing the way you act or think. They affect your attitude about life, yourself, and your opinion of sin. Proverbs 13:20. Too many played religion to try to influence the system for some break. We all had prison officers that we had to report to. The hypocrites hurt the few who were serious, to the point that if one seemed too religious, it was called riding the Bible out. I remember looking out my one small window. I could see the fence, topped with razor wire, and the gun trucks that rode around the outside fence. I had heard of some who made it to the fence. But there was a swamp just across the road.

Those who cleared the fence and made it across the road didn't want to brave the swamp, and they were soon caught. Having been raised in the Everglades, the devil had me convinced that I could make it. Lying down on my bunk, I was looking toward the window, and my mind racing. Could I make it to the swamp? I would have to stay there a few days. Then how was I to arrange my way to my next point? Romans 7:24: "0 wretched man that I am! who shall deliver me from the body of this death?" I wrestled back and forth, back and forth. Try to escape? Or stay put? As the battle was going on in my mind, I remember picking up a paper. I don't remember just what it was, but I believe it was something about end-times in Revelation—maybe a pamphlet from my mother. But I just told God that if he would help me out, I would do something for him, maybe build a church or something like that.

Then something jolted my mind. You don't make deals with God. How foolish people can be, thinking that we can bargain with the one who designed and brought into existence all creation and keeps it running.

The Holy Ghost was making Jesus Christ so real to me. The one I had continually rejected was still seeking me. Yet the spirit was also letting me know that time was running out. I said, "O God, if you will accept someone like me, then I will serve you as I have the devil ... with everything that I've got." And he did.

The devil's plan was colliding with God's mercy. One way that you can tell if someone has been born again, washed in the blood of Jesus, is whether or not there is a complete change—a change in their talk, and they won't go to the places they used to go. The newfound love takes a different outlook. Things look different, and for sure their opinion of sin changes. There is no more little sin or big sin; all sin leads to hell.

Most of all, Jesus died for my sins, a horrible death upon a cross of pain and shame. I didn't want to hurt him anymore. Ephesians 4:30 says, "And grieve not the holy Spirit of God"(whereby ye are sealed unto the day of redemption). Second Corinthians 5:17: "Therefore if any man be in Christ, he is a new creature: old things are passed away behold, all things are become new." Well, he did save me, and though I failed him many times in many ways, never have I thought about turning back. God gives free will to each person, but only a fool would choose hell. I didn't understand the blindness, the deception that was on me. As I lay on the bunk that day, I didn't realize the battle that was going on in my mind—the struggle between life and death. To live, I had to die to the flesh, but it kept fighting to live. God the Holy Ghost was pointing me to Jesus, while the enemy was struggling to keep me in the flesh, to keep my carnal mind focused solely on the things of this world—the lust of the flesh, the lust of the eyes, the pride of life (1 John 2:16).

Friend, if you've ever been in this battle, you know exactly what I'm talking about. Pray that you make the same decision I made that day as I lay on my bunk. I reached under my bunk and got the Bible that my mother had sent me the month before. The KJV Bible that I had hid and was so ashamed of would now become my daily bread. It still amazes me how a man so wicked, so unclean, who had such a hard heart, can be changed into a new man so quickly. How he can become a new creature after the scales have fallen from his eyes. At the conversion of a soul, the Bible says in Acts 9:18, "And immediately there fell from his eyes as it had been scales; and he received sight forthwith, and arose and was baptized."

I wasn't blinded by a bright light of glory as Paul was. But when I confessed my wicked condition and asked my Savior into my heart, it was as if scales had fallen from my eyes. Blinded by sin most of my life, now I could see. As glory entered my heart, the old man died. I was alive from the dead, and my members as instruments of righteousness unto God by his grace.

The Bible says, "For ye are bought with a price; therefore glorify God in your body and in your spirit which are God's" (1 Corinthians 6:20). Things looked so different. It was as if I had stepped into a new world. As the Bible says, I was a born-again child of God. I was no longer conformed to this world but transformed by the renewing of my mind. My conscience had come alive, no longer seared. A peace came over me that this world knows nothing about. Not a temporal peace that is led by a feeling but a peace down in my soul that only comes from Christ. Though storms come and the valleys are deep and wide, I know to keep watching, for somewhere there is a lily in the valley. A loving Father who will lead me through the valley across the deep waters will set me on the other side and then give me credit for it. What a mighty God we serve. The heavens and heavens of heavens can't contain him. The earth is his footstool. He gave me not only life but a hope, an eternal hope. One day soon, I will see my Savior, the one who holds the world in his hand.

I paid little attention and had taken for granted the things in our everyday lives. Many nights, I would be out in my boat, commercial fishing, looking at the moon and the stars, not thinking of how as the moon started to go down, the tide would begin to rise. The night winds would start moving, the oysters would start cracking, and the fish would start jumping, coming ashore with the rising water. Never had I seen God's hand in all of nature. Hebrews 1:3, "Upholding all things by the word of his power." Is that not amazing? God keeps all things in balance and still sees the sparrow that falls and daily loads us with benefits. Is that not a miracle? Born again, no longer a captive of Satan, in prison with a twenty-five-year sentence, I had more freedom than ever.

In the world, I was bound. The guards, the fence with razor wire, and the gun trucks were no longer a threat to my freedom. Yes, they had taken my name and given me a number, 103462, to call over the loudspeaker. But now I would laugh and think, *My name is written in the Lamb's Book of Life.* My earthen parents loved me more than life itself. Now I have a heavenly Father who loves me so much more. He gave his only begotten Son so that I could have the feeling that overflowed my heart—a love that forgave the very man that I sought to harm for being a witness against me. My thoughts changed, and my attitude changed. I could now see; my time in prison was God's way of getting my attention. He is so faithful even in my rebellion. I am so blessed that he loved me so much he prepared this prison for me.

So I started reading my Bible, and if remember right, I read it five times that first year. And it was more than just reading. I was studying it. I was praying for God to teach me his Word and not let me be deceived. Ephesians 5:26 says, "That he might sanctify and cleanse it with the washing of water by the word." I was surely being cleansed by God's Word.

Being born again was surely a miracle, but one must push on—asking, seeking, knocking. I was saved by the blood of Jesus. My sin was gone, as far as the east is from the west. I was a new creature in Christ, and more was to come! When Jesus Christ was on the cross and cried, "It is finished!" he made the way for "whosoever will to walk through this wilderness in total victory" "that he would grant you, according to the riches of his glory, to be strengthened with might by His Spirit in the inner man" (Ephesians 3:16). The child of God will have tribulations, persecution, and troubled times, but by love for and faith in the one that died for them, they will continue going on, not looking back. There's an old saying: trials will make you either better or bitter. He has intended for the fire of these trials to make us stronger in faith, pure in heart.

Isaiah 43:2 says, "When thou passest through the waters, I will be with thee and through the rivers, they shall not overflow thee: when thou walkest through the fire, thou shalt not be burned neither shall the flame kindle upon thee."

I still today teach on hellfire and damnation. I'm sure the fear of hell helped get my attention. For sure, I didn't turn to Christ because I loved Him, for how can you love someone that you don't even know? Probably one reason the different so-called Bibles of today are doing away with hell, and preachers aren't preaching it, is because they want to hide the truth. (Avoid any preacher that does not preach against sin. Remember, it is sin that causes a break in our relationship with God.) Being born again, having Christ within me, I now know for certain that I have his love. My newfound love for Jesus has me serve him with all my heart and soul. To some, my strict walk with God opens me up to being accused of being in works or being a legalist. They don't understand that I walk with unconditional love for the right motives, desiring to please my Father. Holiness to me is a way of life, and in the eyes of God, holiness is essential.

Hebrews 12:14 says, "Follow peace with all men, and holiness, without which no man shall see the Lord." After being born again, in a short time, I was sanctified, which was another great experience. Sanctification is being in strict obedience to God. It is God's will for us to be sanctified. I didn't understand at first what had happened, but as I was walking in the compound, the Lord showed me. I had truly died in the flesh and became as a child, in complete obedience to him. I was truly a babe in Christ, not having a church, pastor, or teacher—only my mother, who could help only by her fervent prayers and her writing.

I was seeking the Holy Ghost, not really knowing what to expect. One afternoon, I was by myself (my roommate was not in), sitting in a chair beside my bunk in our little eight-by-ten cell when God so sweetly blessed me. I remember strange words that came to my mind. I knew the evidence of the Holy Ghost speaking in tongues, but the devil was telling me that I was making it up. I, being ignorant and afraid of being deceived, wouldn't accept it. Of course, God knew that I was truly innocent.

Scripture is clear on the evidence of receiving the Holy Ghost. Mark 16:17: "And these signs shall follow them that believe; In my name shall they cast out devils; they shall speak with new tongues." Acts 10:44: "While Peter yet spake these words, the Holy Ghost fell on all them which heard the word."

How did they know? Acts 10:46: "For they heard them speak with tongues, and magnify God."

I lay in wonder that night. The next morning, my roommate was gone, and I got up, still in wonder, my mind on the Lord when the Holy Ghost came on me. This time, there was no doubt. The new tongue came, and I spoke in the heavenly language for a long while. I often wonder if the guards came by and thought I had lost it. I didn't know if anyone came by or was around, but I didn't care. I was in heaven in that little eight-by-ten cell. I knew I had the special gift of the Holy Ghost, not man given or man taught but full of the person of the Holy Ghost, the third person of the Godhead.

First Corinthians 6:19 says, "What? know ye not that your body is the temple of the Holy Ghost which is in you, which ye have of God, and ye are not your own?"

We are all heading for eternity. The time is short. And Satan as a roaring lion is spreading confusion and deception in a sin-sick world.

One of the first things I remember that God showed me in my new walk was that my mind is a battlefield. The mind is where Satan had access to tempt me, to influence me. I had to learn to be conscience of my mind at all times. I had to learn the voice of the serpent, to check any thoughts and to know that confusion was of the devil. One might ask, How do we check our thoughts or discern right from wrong? How are we to try the spirits? I was praying one day over some thoughts I had. Seemed I had two thoughts, and one thing sounded right, but my conscience was questioning the thought. I was starting to get confused, and then the Lord said for me to try the spirits, leading me to 1 John 4:1: "Beloved, believe not every spirit, but try the spirits whether they are of God." Now, how do we do that? With the Word of God. To be a good soldier, you must be armed. Ephesians 6:17: "And take the helmet of salvation, and the sword of the Spirit, which is the word of God."

When Jesus was tempted in the wilderness, His reply to Satan was with the Word.

Satan has no chance against the Word because the Word is God. John 1:1: "In the beginning was the Word and the Word was with God, and the Word was God." This should give the picture of how well we must know the Word of God—studying it, praying over it, fasting over the Word until we have been enlightened with the true understanding of it. Not living on the opinions of others only but by what we know from God. If you haven't read the Bible from Genesis to Revelation at least once or twice, then you are standing on someone else's opinions. That someone else isn't going to be standing in your place when your eternal destiny is determined. You and you alone will give the account of your life, and it had better been lived according to the Word of God.

Without Jesus Christ in our hearts, we are being led by the spirit of this world. We live in the flesh, the carnal mind, mostly controlled by feelings rather than reason. We live by the following: if it feels good, it must be right. Yet the Bible says in Romans 12:2, "And be not conformed to this world but be ye transformed by the renewing of your mind, that ye may prove what is that good, and acceptable, and perfect, will of God." Romans 8:7: "Because the carnal mind is enmity against God for it is not subject to the law of God, neither indeed can be."

When I talk to different people about their salvation, many will say that we can't live without sin, and they don't even know what sin is. They relate to the thoughts of the mind, such as bad thoughts of a person or the temptations of drinking, smoking, and so on. First, the Bible says sin is the transgression of the law. First John 3:4: "Whosoever committeth sin transgresseth also the law for sin is the transgression of the law." When a person knows something is wrong, yet they go ahead and do it, they have transgressed the law. And again, our mind is where Satan has access. He has the ability to put thoughts in our mind. As a fishing guide, I like the illustration of one throwing a fishing lure in a spot along the shoreline to catch a snook. You may use a white lure, and if that doesn't work, then you try a yellow one. If the color doesn't lure the fish, sometimes the constant beating of the water will provoke him to strike in anger. So it is with the devil. Until a person can "bring into captivity every thought to the obedience of Christ" (2 Corinthians 10:5) through continual discipline, the devil will use your mind to get you to stumble. He knows humans. He watches and listens, because we usually tell him what sins are most appealing to us. Stop and listen to yourself as you talk to your buddies. What are you talking about? Even truth can be gossip. Where do you think Satan is getting the knowledge for the temptations to dangle before us? Sanctified saints don't talk about those things and don't stay around to listen.

So he starts fishing, throwing one lure (thought) after another at us. Until you strike, like the snook going after a lure, he hasn't caught you. In other words, the thoughts he puts in your mind are just thoughts that you either immediately throw out (reject) or conceive by taking a hold of them and thinking further about them. Until you entertain a thought, it is not sin.

Paul said in Romans 6:2, "God forbid, How shall we, that are dead to sin, live any longer therein?"

First John 3:6 says, "Whosoever abideth in him sinneth not:

whosoever sinneth hath not seen him, neither known him." First John 3:8 says, "He that committeth sin is of the devil for the devil sinneth from the beginning." For this purpose, the son of God was manifested, that he might destroy the works of the devil. Jesus was plain about saving his people from their sins. "For he shall save His people from their sins" (Matthew 1:21). The devil loves to converse with you. Yes, he loves an idle mind or a mind numbed by drugs or alcohol. But I learned also that when one tarries too long on even good thoughts, you must be careful. Your guard must be up.

In prison, you have a lot of idle time, so you tend to let your mind wander back home, maybe to your old boat. You think about the old days, leisurely riding through the islands, not a care on your mind. You imagine a beautiful beach with the palm trees, a picture-perfect blue sky, the water so clear. You've relaxed while thinking these thoughts about happier days. But then the devil jumps in. Suddenly a woman appears in the picture, and Satan says, "Remember the time ..." and he begins to talk.

Once again, he has thrown the lure, but this time I recognize it and go on. Second Corinthians 2:11: "Lest Satan should get an advantage of us for we are not ignorant of his devices." Despite my mother and despite that old-time Church of God that had been a light to the community, I knew very little about the Bible. I didn't really understand that I was living only by God's mercy and grace. The Bible states often that His mercy endures forever, but—reader, beware—his grace will run out, and a day of judgment will most certainly occur, perhaps sooner than you expect.

Looking back, I believe I was at that very time in my life when it was either accept God or be doomed forever. It still stirs my heart today, because the choice I made was between God and the world, heaven and hell.

My soul was battling for life—a life where my sins would be forgiven for the sake of Jesus atoning sacrifice at Calvary and the blood that he shed. A life where I could call the first person of the triune Godhead my Father, and a life where I yielded to the Holy Ghost. The old Vernon surely didn't want to die, didn't want to be crucified. My flesh, my old self, blinded by the so-called pleasure of this sin-loving world, wanted to retain the yoke of Satan and the bondage of sin and shut my eyes to the certain punishment of a lake of fire. As Paul writes in Romans 6:8, "Now if we be dead with Christ, we believe that we shall also live with Him."

By the grace of God, I asked Jesus to save me, and if He would, then I would serve Him as I had served the devil—with my all. In just a couple of weeks, I was saved, sanctified, Holy Ghost filled. The old Vernon had died, and a new man, one that neither my family nor old acquaintances knew, had been born. In fact, I didn't know myself. Just a few days before, I was in total despair—no life left, depressed, angry, no hope, ready to tear a guy's head off for the smallest thing.

Now I was excited, full of life, and with hope that is eternal. If I died in prison, heaven was going to be my home. I would see Jesus my Savior, the one who died for me and gave me great salvation.

Romans 6:5 says, "For if we have been planted together in the likeness of his death, we shall be also in the likeness of his resurrection." Polk Correction was a big place. There was a clothes factory, a medical facility (or facilities?), and a tech school. One of the dorms was just for people with medical conditions. In the middle of the compound was the kitchen/dining area and a place for worship. All inmates had to have a job, and it was approved by their counsellor. These people were ones you went to for advice, for jobs, for gain time—how much time you had or when you might be eligible for work release. All of these free men and women came in each day and had offices and places where they ate and hung out. Our gain time depended a lot on our jobs. My roommate worked among these free people, doing some cleaning, running to and fro as a messenger. I had gotten a job with electrical maintenance, which was a real blessing.

My boss was a free man professing to be a Christian. Being on this team of about six or eight men, I had access in and out of the dorms. Lots of time for reading and praying. When the free man's contract came up, another man came in who I liked a lot. We became friends. He was good at his job and taught me a lot—enough that when I did get to work release some years later, I got a job with Pete's Electric in Ft. Myers. I worked with them for about nine months with good standing.

Now I had given my life to God, and my whole outlook on life had changed, and I tried to explain this the best I could to my roommate. He knew I had changed and maybe wasn't too surprised when I told him the weed and the money had to go. I no longer wanted anything to do with it. He said I should take the money and that he'd take the weed. I said, "No. I don't want any of either. Just have it gone. If it's up to me, it will all be flushed down the toilet."

I told him that I would apply for another room, which took a little while. During this time, I talked to him about the Lord. You could tell that these talks touched his heart. How sad it was to see him with tears in his eyes. He agreed that I was right, but he just couldn't give in, just couldn't surrender himself. As far as I know, he never did break loose from the bondage of sin, and only God knows what happened later in his life. But the seed of truth had been planted. I changed rooms on good terms, with no hard feelings between us.

Over the years, I have talked to many like my roommate, and I understand the battle. He knew I was right but was held captive. It's as if the soul is crying for help, but the flesh, in its weakness to sin, just won't give in. Only by the blood can it be put to death or under subjection.

A short time before Jesus went to the cross, in the garden, he told His disciples, as it says in Matthew 26:41, "Watch and pray, that ye enter not into temptation the spirit indeed is willing, but the flesh is weak." True conversion, true change in every aspect of one's life. When Jesus Christ comes into the heart, everything else has to go!

Before I was born again, there was a man named Paul, a black man, a little over six feet, slender and with the biggest, loudest mouth you've ever heard. If the prison's PA system broke down, you could have hooked the speakers up to his mouth, and the entire prison would have heard the message. I would hear him when he came into the dorm from my upstairs room. No one was supposed to come in except if you lived there or had a good excuse. But Paul would come in and seemed to shout at everyone down the halls, up the stairs. I told my friend that I was thinking of stopping that loud mouth. He said, "Be careful. You get in trouble in here, you would lose your room." Well, Paul was sent to another prison or back to county jail for some reason. In the time that he was gone, I got saved and moved downstairs to my new room.

One day while settled in my room, I heard that old familiar voice. Right away, I knew it was Paul, but the voice had a different ring. It didn't have a sound of arrogance. I met Paul, and in talking to him, he told me how he had also been saved before his return. We became good friends. He would come over, and we would kneel down together on the cement floor by my bunk and pray. We prayed together, laughed together, and sometimes cried together. I told Paul how I used to get so mad at him and his loud mouth. He would laugh and say, "Brother Vernon, it's loud now for Jesus!"

You can put a little of Jesus in the most hardened heart, and it will break down and become as a little innocent child. Ephesians 5:1 says, "Be ye therefore followers of God, as dear children."

One day, one of the inmates came to my room and said, "Vernon,

Mr. Berry is outside and wants to see you." The inmate told me that I wouldn't recognize him. He had lost so much weight and was very sick, very weak. And he was right; this once-big man was skin and bones. I walked him over to a bench, and he began to tell me how he had become sick, and the doctors had given him about three months to live. Since Polk Prison had the medical dorm and doctors, they sent him there to die. It was about thirty years ago, but from what I remember, he had a tumor that had grown around a main artery. He was very weak.

He asked me how I was doing, and I told him great and that I had good news. He immediately said, "They lowered your custody."

"No, Mr. Berry, not that. I got saved. I turned my life to Jesus."

He looked at me for a moment and said, "I knew there was something different about you."

"Yes, Mr. Berry, I've settled down now that I've given all over to the Lord. And more good news—God heals too."

We talked for a short time, and he asked me to help him to the dorm, saying, "Vernon, I want to hear more about this."

The next morning, I went and got Mr. Berry, and we sat outside. I told him all about Jesus, how he died for our sins and how he was beaten before heading to the cross—beaten so viciously that his innards were hanging out, but by those stripes we were healed. Each day, I tried to spend time with him, talking about the Lord. After seeing the change in me and knowing that that change was true, from the heart, he said he would like to be saved, so we prayed, and he gave his life to God. As always, through Jesus Christ and with him in control, things change. Mr. Berry's countenance had changed. He was laughing as he walked through the valley of the shadow of death. He seemed to be gaining a little weight, and we began walking a little farther.

One day, we went over toward a building in a shady place, and we were praying. I felt as though God had touched Mr. Berry. In fact,

I just knew God had healed him. I said, "Mr. Berry, for a man that doesn't have but a month more to live, you sure are doing good." He was gaining weight. His strength had improved so much that now we were walking around the whole track.

The doctors called him in because they couldn't believe his progress. They examined him, took x-rays, and had to admit the tumor was gone. Mr. Berry came to me, saying, "I've got the proof! It's gone! I'm healed!" We were so excited. Mr. Berry must have told everyone in the whole compound how God had healed him. He sure spread the word and was soon released and went home. There is proof in the Bible that God is still in the healing business. Matthew 8:17 says, "That it might be fulfilled which was spoken by Esaias the prophet, saying, Himself took our infirmities, and bare our sicknesses."

Psalm 103:3: "Who forgiveth all thine iniquities; who healeth all thy diseases."

Isaiah 53:5: "But he was wounded for our transgressions, he was bruised for our iniquities the chastisement of our peace was upon him and with his stripes we are healed."

Many times since then, I have seen and heard of healing. God has healed me many times, and my daughter and many in the church. God has not changed. He still saves, and he still heals. It's people—even those who confess Jesus—who have changed. They have turned to unbelief regarding his power over every single aspect of life. The same God that can save a wretched sinner is the same Almighty God that can destroy tumors, eliminate cancer, heal hearts, and make our physical body whole. Shouldn't it be obvious that the same God who created us also has the power to heal us?

Our creator knows the thoughts, even the intents of the heart. He knows the motive. He sees if his Word is in the heart or the intellect.

Obadiah 1:3–4 quotes, "The pride of thine heart hath deceived thee, thou that dwellest in the clefts of the rock, whose habituation is high, that saith in his heart, who shall bring me down to the ground? Though thou exalt thyself as the eagle and though thou set thy nest among the stars thence will I bring thee down, saith the Lord."

They were so convinced that no one could bring them from the clefts of the rocks that they became deceived, maybe bragging to one another how wise they were living in the rocks—how untouchable they had become, giving all glory to themselves instead of God. They never thought of God, who gave them the clefts. The Almighty God that gives takes at his will. All things are of God, and he controls all things. We deceive ourselves into thinking we hold things in our hands, at our will. It's pride in our deceived hearts that makes us think we control instead of the power of God, creator of all things. He even discerns the intentions of the heart. It's pride of heart, being full of self, that makes us believe we control anything. Our next breath is in his hands.

Yet we have pride enough to think we control our wealth, our health, even our being. The pride of our hearts won't let us admit that we are not our own, and we can do nothing without Christ. Oh we do many things, but without Christ, it's all vanity, all in vain, empty. How foolish to earn our way into eternal hell. Romans 6:23: "For the wages of sin is death; but the gift of God is eternal life through Jesus Christ our Lord." The pride of my heart would say, "Look at how smart I am, how strong I was, how I overcame those seeking my life." Oh foolish one I was. It was God's grace, his mercy that kept me from being crushed, destroyed at any given moment. Only by the blood of Jesus, being born again, were my eyes opened. Once in darkness, now in light; once a heart of stone, now a heart of flesh. I look at my blinded past with tears—tears I can now shed. I am ashamed but also proud in a godly way to see and admit how weak I was. How stupid to be led so easily by the devil, when my Lord was there all the time.

My intention in this testimony is not in any way to glorify one in sin or criminal activity. My desire is to point out how easily one can be deceived and become so prideful they lose sight and become blind to the truth. To be so weak to the lure of the devil that they fall right into his plan to destroy. My desire is to tell my testimony in hopes someone can see themselves and realize the path they are on. Jesus told the disciples that the spirit is indeed willing, but the flesh is weak. If the devil has you following his plan or if you feel the pull, remember, God's mercy is always ready to deliver. His grace is pulling, but it's your freewill choice to accept or refuse it. God's great long-suffering love is waiting. His so great salvation is for whoever will let him come.

Sometime after being born again, I was able to move to another room. Not that I had anything against my roommate, but I knew the time was right for me to move. It was a room downstairs where I would be for the rest of my stay in max security. I was still a babe in Christ, and knowing the danger of deception, I stayed to myself as much as I could. I spent all the time I could reading my Bible and praying. My mother would write to me and answer my questions. As I began to get out more and witness to others, I could see that out of nine hundred men in max security, I was one of the few who was guilty of a crime. Most of the other men were full of excuses and blaming others for their crimes. Most would confess a love for God, and a large number would say that they were Christians. Is the world today any different? Just as in the world, the prison was full of religion. I will say that many of those men surely knew the Bible and could quote scripture. But Satan himself knows the Bible (James 2:19), "Thou believers that there is one God; thou doest well; the devils also believe and tremble." They believe and tremble, but their hearts are far from God.

I didn't have a church, a pastor, or true fellowship with a brother, but I had what counts to anyone who lives truth. I had God's holy

Word and the Holy Ghost to teach me. All I had to do was to study the Word on my knees with a willing heart open to truth. Scriptures such as Psalm 101:3, "I will set no wicked thing before mine eyes; I hate the works of them that turn aside. It shall not cleave to me." It didn't thirty years ago, and by the grace of God it won't now. Things that at one time would embarrass us now are turned loose to our children. They see and are open to more filth in one hour than most of us elders were in years.

One of the highlights of my selfish stupidity was to let my son have one of my beers. What a poor example of a so-called man to drink anywhere, but most of all before his wife and children. Alcohol and drugs ruin the mind and blind the eyes of one who has good intentions. Proverbs 7:10: "And behold, there met him a woman with the attire of a harlot, and subtil of heart."

What is the attire of a harlot? In my past life of sin, I could tell you. But now, even ones confessing to be Christian expose more of their body than most of the harlots I knew. Yes, times have changed, but God hasn't. You can yield to the styles, changes of the world, but God's Word still stands. All I read about saints in heaven is spotless robes of white and on earth modest apparel. First Timothy 2:9 says, "In like manner also, that women adorn themselves in modest apparel, with shamefacedness and sobriety, not with broided hair, or gold, or pearls, or costly array."

I started going to a few church meetings, as some group would come in and hold a service. Most of the time, I didn't know who or what church group it was until I got there, and then it would be too late. The guards would take the ones who wanted to go, and you couldn't leave until the service was over.

Going around the compound and to some of the meetings, I began to know some of the men who were interested in salvation. I had talked to my roommate about Jesus and how Christ had changed my life. He turned his life to Jesus, so when I started having different ones come to my room for Bible study, he was all in favor.

One young man who started coming by was a Catholic. David would come and had his beads he called a Rosary. He came for several meetings, and I started talking to him about his life on earth and then eternity. I spent a lot of time with this young man, and he would cry and tell me about his life before prison. He had caught his wife with an off-duty policeman at a gas station, and in a struggle with the policeman, this young man took his gun, and the policeman took off in a car. "Vernon," he said, "I was out of my mind. I emptied the gun, and one bullet struck my wife and killed her." He is now in prison for life. He was quiet and mostly stayed by himself. Out on the compound, I would walk the track with him or sit and talk. It took a while for him to understand that you don't confess your sin to man. He didn't understand Jesus Christ had suffered and died for our sins, and Jesus was our high priest. We are to go to Jesus for all our needs. Mary was a good woman, truly a virgin and with a special calling, but she is not the one we worship. It's all about Jesus our Savior. He is the one and only that we worship and give our praises too. The light turned on, and David gave his all to Jesus. When I finally left the prison, David was still with Jesus.

I thank God the Father for sending his only begotten Son, born of a virgin. I thank God the Son, born of a virgin. I thank God the Son for coming to save his people from their sins. I thank God the Holy Ghost for his comfort, his teaching, and always pointing to Christ.

Now I'll tell you about a man named Al. Al was in the same dorm as I was. After I moved downstairs and started getting out, I met him. He knew the Bible well, and we agreed on scripture more than anyone else I had met. The year and a half or two that I knew him, I never knew what he was in prison for. He didn't talk about his past. I don't even know if he had been married or had any children. I had my ideas, but they were never confirmed. Most of the men had either wives, children, brothers, or sisters to come visit. But I don't remember Al ever going to the visit park. I met so many men in prison who knew the Bible so well to be in the shape they were in. But I did notice, after getting to spend time with them, that somewhere in scripture they would be way off in some points. A lot of those men are the same as people I talk to now out on the streets. They think or act like they believe because at one time in their life they were baptized or said some prayer that they were saved, and they think they would go to heaven if they died. They won't accept the facts, that if they were ever saved, they for sure have backslid. They refuse to accept that they are on their way to hell and need to confess their sins and repent. The once-saved-always-saved Calvinist doctrine is a lie that has deceived many.

Another man I met, I believe his name was Jim, lived in the open dorms. I met him out on the compound. He wasn't in very long, but the short time I knew him, he seemed to be a decent man with good morals. That may sound strange to say a good man with good morals is in prison. For all the ones in prison, there are many more who just haven't been caught—maybe someone you know or even hang out with. Of the many men I met and talked to, I could mostly tell the ones who had a good background or knew they were wrong in their choice in life. Some were ashamed, some were sorry they had been caught, and some just didn't care and were proud of their ungodly lifestyle.

Jim's wife would come visit. The place for visitors was small, with a few tables and chairs. My mother and dad came almost every weekend. So we met Jim's wife. She seemed to be a nice lady, and my mother took to her right from the start. Mother, the way she was, never met a stranger. With her big smile, she would talk to anyone. She would pray for anyone, anytime, anyplace. They became friends and stayed in touch for a long time.

Jim and I talked about the Bible. We talked about the goodness of God, but we didn't agree on many things. I guess one thing that kept me talking with him was that I felt he was sincere but mixed up. Instead of faith, was trying to serve God in works. One in works gets frustrated in their up and down walk and keeps striving to find peace in the things they keep trying to overcome, not realizing they are not truly giving all to God but in their own way are trying to have salvation. He reminds me of Romans 7:15, "For that which I do I allow not; for what I would, that do I not; but what I hate that do I."

We were talking one day, and I asked him, "Jim, do you believe smoking is a sin?" He said yes. I said, "Then why do you keep smoking?" Sin can never enter heaven. If you are born again, crucified with Christ, then your flesh, your selfish self is dead. Romans 6:10–11: "For in that he died, he died unto sin once: but in that he liveth unto God—likewise (same for us) reckon he also yourselves to be dead indeed unto sin but alive unto God through Jesus Christ our Lord."

Romans 6:2: "God forbid. How shall we that are dead to sin live any longer therein?"

Jim said that he was trying to stop smoking, that it was really hard. I told him, "No, you're not trying to quit." He looked at me in surprise. I said, "Jim, if you are trying to stop smoking, why are you carrying them around in your pocket with a lighter?"

He thought about it a few minutes and then said, "I guess you are right."

One thing we must learn quickly in our prayer life and fellowship with God is always be honest—first with God and second with yourself. The flesh doesn't die easily. It will try to overrule the Word of God, make excuses, make a deal, lie, anything but completely die.

I believe Jim, as so many others, wanted salvation and the habit as well. He had deceived himself. The flesh wasn't dead.

Romans 7:18: "For I know that in me (that is, in my flesh) dwelleth no good thing: for to will is present with me; but how to perform that which is good I find not." Only by grace through faith (not works) is there victory in Jesus Christ.

My little brother Doyle, Mother Betty and my two small girls.

Smallwood Store and School Boat

CHAPTER 3

I SPENT SEVERAL MONTHS in county jail before going to Lake Butler. I was in a cell with a man who had been in and out of prison and knew the system. He told me what to expect since I had never been in prison before. He said that because of my age and the fact I looked like someone who wouldn't take anything from anyone, I probably wouldn't have any trouble getting settled in. When I finally reached my destination some months later, I saw what he was talking about.

The Bluebird bus pulled up in front of the prison, Polk Correction, where there was a cage made of fence wire with metal on top. From the bus, we went into the cage, and there they took our chains off. I was now at my new home, where I was to spend the next few years. The devil I'm sure thought all was in his hands, that his plan for my destruction was coming to a quick end. He had heard my talk with others. He had watched my attitude and knew the hardness of my heart. I guess Satan's deception is so great and his hate for God and his creation is so strong that maybe he forgets God's mercy. He was so sure of his plan for me he must have overlooked mercy. Mercy got off the bus, and mercy followed me into the prison. Mercy was just waiting for that exact moment of my life when I was finally so broken, with nowhere to turn, at my wit's end. Mercy would step in and reveal Jesus Christ by the Holy Ghost, and by grace, I would be saved.

We exited the cage into the prison compound, and the guards led us down the main entrance of the prison, a narrow road where the supply trucks came through the double gates, mainly to a factory called Pride.

As I walked down the narrow road, the visiting park was on my left, and the office building and medical building were on my right. I could hear the big gates closing behind, and I think maybe it was then my hope left and reality came in. I had always gotten what I wanted. I did what I wanted, when I wanted. I was a selfish man with a false hope without God. I hadn't been too upset about the twenty-five-year sentence until now. I had an attorney still working on my case. But I hadn't heard from anyone in several months. Loneliness and depression covered my very soul. My mother and dad seemed to be all I had in the world, and as I came closer to the cons of the convicts, I knew from my past that I was about to be tried, and I could show no weakness. I had been warned about getting into trouble. Some men had come to prison with a year or two sentence, but getting into trouble cost them more time. Some ended up with many years. I didn't have much patience, and my fuse was short, but I was in a different world and had no control of the situation. I had to be tough but smart in a worldly manner.

The cons I refer to are the group of men standing by waiting for a van or bus of new prisoners. They may be known as the greeting team. They are not there for friendly reasons but always for selfish desires. One reason is to greet ones who may be transferred from another prison. The transferred carry greetings from one prison to another. To a good number of the inmates, the system is a game to them. Their time is short, and they have friends and become heroes to the younger ones on the streets.

The main reason for meeting the newcomers is to see what they can con them out of. Those who have never spent time in prison are the ones they really like to greet, especially young boys. The young men who haven't been in before usually will have money sent to their banks in the prison that they can draw out for the canteen. The con, knowing you don't have any money on you and won't for a short time, will try to buy you a drink, candy, or a smoke. Then later when you draw, they will remind you how helpful they were when you first came in. And if they refuse the offer, they turn their tough side, wanting to know why you are so unfriendly and don't appreciate their kindness. Most of these newcomers are afraid, not knowing what to expect. *Webster's* defines *con*: "To swindle (a victim) by first gaining his confidence."

The object of the cons was to get these newcomers thinking they owed them favors. The con wants to have an errand boy or one to help him with his habits by giving him money. In his filthy pride, he would score good among his friends if he turned one into his mate.

I never had any problems with the cons or any inmates. I was angry at times. My temper rose but never got me into trouble. Prison was a lot like the streets. The tough ones didn't cause any trouble, and the others just wanted people to think they were tough.

After I had been in prison a while and was saved, I and others would try to help the newcomers. We would take them under our wing, so to speak, try to be with them as much as we could. But these men, being in the open dorms at lockdown from evening until the next morning, were in a constant battle. We helped a few, and some got into a group themselves and overcame. I remember a few good turnouts, but I also remember some troublesome ones.

As I write now, looking back at prison and the years before, and even now at my surroundings, what a clear picture of the two worlds we live in—one ruled by Satan and the real world, the spiritual world, ruled by God. Satan's world is selfishness, pride, no hope, all things temporal, and certain destruction with judgment from God—the eternal lake of fire.

Now, as a born-again child of God, it's strange for me to write and try to explain things I went through in a devil's world without God. The words such as *tough* and *bad* and sayings such as *only sissies cry*—I see now the blindness of the deception that was on me. And I see the truth of such a wasted life—thinking I was tough and strong when it was weakness. Anyone can serve the devil. It takes a real man to humble himself and serve the Living God.

The biggest con you will ever meet is the devil. He will lie to you, promise you things that are all temporary, and tell you that you don't have to live that way, that you have plenty of time—don't worry about eternity now. Religion is all right; just don't go too far. But remember, he is the master of all cons.

Vision of the Valley

I suppose that to most people today, the word *valley* has no special meaning. But to a child of God, the thoughts that quickly pass through the mind are *trials, persecution, troubles*. We talk about being in a valley or going through a valley—sometimes forgetting the must for the valley.

Second Timothy 3:12–13 says, "Yea and all that will live godly in Christ Jesus shall suffer persecution." Those who are mature in Christ know the valleys we go through teach us many things. They increase our faith and patience, and it's how we grow. First Peter 4:12 says, "Beloved think it not strange concerning the fiery trial which is to try you as though some strange thing happened unto you. But rejoice inasmuch as ye are partakers of Christ sufferings, that, when his glory shall be revealed, ye may be glad also with exceeding joy."

Valleys are brought up in many places in scripture. Isaiah 22:1 brings up the burden of the valley of vision. In verse 5 of the chapter, he says, "For it is a day of trouble and of treading down and of perplexity by the Lord God of hosts in the valley of vision breaking down the walls and of crying to the mountains." Ezekiel 37 talks about the valley of dry bones. Psalm 23:4 says, "Yea though I walk through the valley of the shadow of death, I will fear no evil; for thou art with me; thy rod and thy staff they comfort me."

There was comfort in the valley even as the shadow of death came down. Why? Jesus was there. He had already gone before and overcome death. In the Song of Solomon, he speaks of Jesus in 2:1: "I am the rose of Sharon and the Lily of the valley."

We, as children of God, sing about valleys, testify of valleys, and most of the time relate them to trials and persecution. I want to share my vision of a valley. I feel God was showing me his great love, grace, and mercy he has for humankind. His long-suffering of reaching out for each one of His creatures. The Holy Ghost revealed Christ our Savior, always careful not to override the free will he has given us. I believe God was showing me the final choice I was to make before grace was lifted from me. My freewill choice, God or the world. Heaven or hell. It was my decision.

God showed me several things, but what I want to share starts with me in a valley. It was a dense, thick forest. I slowly made my way through, checking out the different plants and the beauty of the flowers. I came into a small clearing. This clearing was at the foot of a cliff. As I was standing and looking up, I saw a ledge along the top of this cliff. The next thing I knew, I was sitting on the ledge overlooking the valley. Only now the valley was no longer a forest, but it was clear, and to the left, I saw a crowd of people. As they came my way up the valley, they broke up into groups until they ended up single file below the ledge where I was sitting. They marched on, one after the other group, as they made their way up the valley. They seemed to be having a good time, laughing and talking, so unconcerned. I saw one man in the group that was having a good time. He must be the life of the party, I thought, as he talked with a drink in his hand, and the others gathered around. But they were coming to a place where the groups started breaking off and marching single file. My eyes were on that certain man as he reached the point of change, and I cried out, "O Lord! That's me!" At that instant, a hand reached down, picked me up, and set me on the ledge. I sat watching the people, so many reaching the point of no return. I now realized the single file ones had no hope, and the cliff they marched over dropped into hell.

It's almost thirty years ago, and I still remember the vision clearly. I still have a fear of how close I was to the point of no return. Grace has a thin line for each of us. Where are you today? How much longer can you reject God? How close are you to the point of no return? Joel 3:14 says, "Multitudes multitude in the valley of decision; for the day of the Lord is near in the valley of decision."

> Because I have called, and ye refused; I have stretched out my hand, and no man regarded; But ye have set at nought all my counsel, and would none of my reproof; I also will laugh at your calamity; I will mock when your fear cometh (and it will come).

> When your fear cometh as desolation, and your destruction cometh as a whirlwind; when distress and anguish cometh upon you. Then shall they call upon

me, but I will not answer; they shall seek me early, but
they shall not find me. (Proverbs 1:24-28)

A short time after my sentencing on May 29, 1986, I hired a new
attorney. He talked with me and after looking over my case filed for
appeal. The appeal was for a new trial and at the least to lower my
sentence slot to the fifteen-year minimum mandatory sentence that I
should have received to begin with.

After about one year and seven months, we heard from the court:
"We vacate the prison sentence and remain with directions to impose
the minimum mandatory sentence of fifteen years. It is not necessary
for the defendant to be present for resentencing."

What the appeal court said was they denied me a new trial, but the
trial court erred in my sentence and was to resentence me with fifteen
years, and I didn't have to go back to Pinellas County courthouse.

We would have to make another appeal for a new trial, but with
my sentence dropped, it would mean that immediately my custody
would be lowered, and I would be sent to work release. I had been
saved now for about a month or two, and now it looked like I would
be going to work release any day. I finally got the call over the speaker
to report to the office. But when I got there, they told me to get my
things together, that I had to go to court back in Pinellas County. I
was disappointed, knowing it wasn't supposed to be. But now I had
God in my life, and as part of my brokenness and his grace, I leaned
on him for help.

During my time in the prison system, there was overcrowding. The
system was so overcrowded that at times they would load the busses
with prisoners and ride them around to keep the numbers down. They
were warned of when the inspectors were coming and would put them
in transit because those in transit weren't counted.

From what I have seen in the prison system, the purpose is not to stop crime but to fulfill a political agenda. Most of the men I met were in and out constantly. Being in prison was just a time-out. It was as if they were out playing hard at their game and needed a rest. I knew one young man who was about to be released, and when I said I was happy for his release, he said, "I'll see you later. I'll be back." There would be a different outlook on prison if they came in and were handed a shovel and marched outside from early until dark. It wouldn't be a worldly camp meeting. In my humble opinion, the system doesn't reform, and to most, it's not even punishment.

In the midst of the overcrowded system, I was sent to the county jail in Pinellas by the trial judge. The county jail was so overcrowded I had to sleep on the floor for the first few nights. I was in what I call a cell block. It wasn't one cell with two to four men. This was like a big cage with bunks at the bottom and a second floor with bunks all in a U shape. The middle part was open so as to provide a small walking space. At mealtime, the guards would wheel carts down the hallways, stopping at each cell. The cells had small slots in the iron doors with a small shelf to slide the plate into the cell, as each inmate would take his meal. This worked well for the cells with two to four men, but in the cell block, it was different. Anytime you put more than two inmates together, especially a dozen or more, there is always the wise guy—the one who always wants to be the chief, the boss. One always complains or causes trouble or is just a loudmouth. I know you find these in the world, but in lockup, you have to put up with them a certain amount. I had been there a couple of days and knew a few of the men. I noticed that at mealtime after the plates had been given out, several of the men didn't get their meal. One of them was a young man in his teens.

Somewhere during this time, a bunk came open for me upstairs. I was glad for the bunk, even though it was a thin mat on a metal sheet. It was much better than sleeping on the concrete floor—nowhere to rest during the day and at night having people stepping on you. Lying on the mat, I thanked God for the bunk. I was still upset about the meals. I had shared my plate with the young man downstairs, but I wondered how long it would go on. As I think back on this time, it surely confirms how true salvation changes a person. I was saved, sanctified, and Holy Ghost filled but still a babe in Christ, maybe now two or three months old. I made my mind to go down and stop the stealing of the plates. I knew what they were doing. Instead of each man getting his own plate, they would form a line, but a couple of the men would stay at the door, and as the food came, they would pass the plates out as they wished, of course keeping a couple extras for themselves.

Confronting the men was no big deal for me; I had faced much more. My surprise was working myself. My anger wasn't controlling my thoughts. In fact, I don't think I was angry. I was calmly talking to my friend about this situation. I was waiting on reason instead of going by feeling as I did in the past.

I've nothing against feeling. I love when I feel God, when my emotions are stirred by his presence. But I don't want to be guided by feelings. They can be so deceiving, so easily led by the flesh.

As I recall that day, it seems impossible now that I was so innocent as a child in Christ, so ignorant of the scriptures, to think that on the one hand I had in mind to even whip a man but then on the other hand consult with a holy God about the matter. But God, being faithful as he is and knowing all things, knew I was sincere and willing to obey. Isn't a willing heart what sanctification is all about?

In my short experience of serving the loving God, this was the first time that I remember him speaking to my heart. I don't remember the exact words, but it was in this manner: "My son." His words were so soft and understanding. "I died for those men, just as I died for you. You are looking at the flesh and the wrong they are doing. I look at the soul that is crying out for help. You, my son, must see them as I do. Look beyond the flesh and see a soul crying for help, the flesh in its weakness will drag the soul into eternal hell. If they reject my grace, then I will reject them in my judgment."

I was surely on top of the mountain for a while. I know the changes in my heart and soul. I knew the deep feelings I had after my born-again experience. But now the almighty God taking the time to lead me to teach me, was overwhelming.

What is faith but to trust and have confidence in Jesus Christ? I think this was one of the many lessons of having to learn to trust and have confidence in the all faithful God, taking all things to him in every aspect of my journey. Proverbs 3:5–6 says, "Trust in the Lord with all thine heart; and lean not unto thine own understanding. In all thy ways acknowledge him and he shall direct thy paths." It wasn't easy praying for those men then and, many times after, praying for those I was in conflict with. But I would pray to my Father in Jesus's name. Simply and honestly, I would pray, "Father, I don't think I even mean these prayers for them, but I will keep praying until I do." Eventually, I would feel peace and a clear conscience. I knew that as a newborn child of God, to be honest and open with him and with myself was the most important thing I could do or learn.

My day of court finally came. I didn't get to speak with them, but my mother and dad were there. They had flown to my hearing with my attorney, and it was their first plane ride. I was the last to be heard in court that day, and I was kept behind bars until the judge said to bring me into the courtroom. The judge already knew what my outcome was going to be; it was obvious. I stood before her, and after her short speech, she let us know that she didn't care what the appeal court said; she held firm to the twenty-five-year sentence. My attorney tried to reason with the court but to no avail.

To have my sentence overturned, my attorney had presented to the appeals court four things that the judge and court had erred in. Surely she knew I would get my sentence lowered, but she also knew it would take the paperwork at least another year. I'm sure when the judge dropped her hammer down, she thought for sure there would be a response of crying or maybe even cursing in some kind of rage. Anything but just looking her in the eyes and smiling.

Little did she know that the man standing before her in handcuffs and leg irons was not the same man she had sentenced several years before. This new man knew after only a few months that God was in complete control, that circumstances would not affect him.

Back in the holding cell, my attorney came to talk with me. He was sorry for the outcome but said he would get back to the appeals court as soon as possible. He knew they would take care of the sentencing, and he said that he was still confident that he could have my trial overturned. I thanked him for his hard work and told him not to proceed in the new trial. I let him know I had been saved and it was all in God's hands now. I didn't say any more, for how do people understand what true repentance does to a soul? I knew deep down now that it was by God's love that I was where I was, and when the time came, he would open the door.

Alone now in the holding cell, tears came and a hurt that only God and I knew. Only this time, the tears and the hurt weren't for myself. It was for the family who loved me so much. My mother and dad, never having been on a plane before, climbed aboard just for me. My selfishness, my rejection of God, was continuing to break their hearts. The selfish words would sing for years: "It's my life. I'll live as

I want." I'll never understand in this lifetime how God could forgive someone like me.

They took me back to my cell, where I would wait a few more weeks before being transferred back to Polk Correction. Being away from the prison as long as I was, it was only the grace of God I got my room back. I was glad to get back to where I could have some private time. Being on the electric maintenance, I had a lot of free time. I would read, pray, and study the Bible every day. The days went by, and then after about a year and a half, it finally happened. I heard over the intercom, "Number 103462, report to the office."

I was right down the hall from the office. When I got there, they said, "Hey, get your things together. You are going to work release."

I was excited to walk through the prison gates with no handcuffs, no chains. I got into a van, and they took me to a dorm where I would stay until they took me to a work release center. The atmosphere was so much better, and the food was great compared to what I was used to. My boss, who was a free man, came to the prison each day and was easy to work for. He knew I spent a lot of time reading and studying my Bible, so he let me off a lot and had it arranged so I could go into the dorm at any time. He knew I was about to go to work release and told me when I got out there, he would come pick me up and drive me around the prison in his truck. After about a week, he did just that. We rode around the outside of the prison. He took me to the warehouse, where all the supplies were. When one of the lights around the prison wall went out, we would take a boom-truck and change the bulbs. Closing in at about five years I was now high above the razor wire, looking into the prison where once I stood by a small window looking out, planning in my confused mind to try to escape. Could I get over the fence before the gun truck saw me? Thank God again for saving my soul.

It wasn't long before I was sent to a work release over in Pinellas County, still hours from home. The work release was a hard-to-explain situation. For one, I didn't work with a boss I thought so much of. The man over me now seemed to be trying me. I was put on twenty-four-hour maintenance, plus watching over a garden the center had. One day, he called me to his office and handed me a driver's handbook and told me to be ready to take a driver's test. He wanted me to drive the work-release van to take workers out and pick them up in the evening, and I didn't know anything about the area. I hadn't driven a car in five years. I wasn't there but a couple months before they finally moved me to Fort Myers work release about seventy-five miles from home.

In just a couple weeks, I got a job with Pete's Electric in Ft. Myers. Back in civilian garments, working among the public gives a feeling of being something you really are not. You feel free while working, then back to reality, back to the work camp. You receive your paycheck as others, and then back at the camp, you hand it over to them. Then after they take their share, they put your part in their holding. I'm not complaining about their share for my keeping, but I mention it to bring to mind the up-and-down feeling of almost free but not. Maybe that is what a sinner feels when under heavy conviction. They can feel and almost see freedom but are still bound—about to break loose, but something is holding you back.

Work release is like giving a child a piece of candy and telling them they can't eat it until later. Some can't resist the temptation and go ahead and eat the candy, knowing the outcome will not be good. The same with sinners. They can't resist the world, its temporal pleasure, even if it means facing eternity later on in rebellion to God. Too many people want the pleasures of the world for a season regardless of the consequences.

After nine months with Pete's Electric, I informed them of my coming release. They wished me the best and, knowing I wasn't staying around, assured me that I always had a job with them.

May 4, 1992. The day had come. I was leaving. I was now a free man, both in the world and in spirit. Pulling out of the driveway, I must have thanked God for leaving, but I also thanked him then and many times since for the place in prison that he had prepared for me.

Our guide Boat-- Nepenthe

Nepenthe and skiff boat with a fishing party.

CHAPTER 4

BEING AN ALCOHOLIC most of my life, I feel I must express my concern and pray that God will shake someone and awake them from this bondage of Satan himself. Drinkers are full of excuses. Drink to be social, to self-medicate to calm the nerves, to have fun. The truth is it destroys the body, soul, and mind.

Most of my drinking was to be social. Most people would never suspect that I had more than a couple of drinks, although I always had a drink or beer in my hand or close by. Whatever I did, wherever I went, the drink had to be in the center. I didn't go out to eat if they didn't serve drinks. It started as a false comfort but soon became my master.

I have known all kinds of alcoholics—all the way from the hardworking men to ditch falling (ditch falling is one who may go weeks without a drink, but after they have a couple of drinks, they may go weeks drunk) to the ones who wear a fancy suit and tie. Yet when their master took over, they slurred their words and cursed, regardless of their backgrounds. We are quick to call them drunks only when they reach a certain point.

It's sad that we rate drinkers from one to ten when they all drink from the same well. Some seem to control it better, when in reality there is no control. Satan is at the wheel. He will start you out thinking you have things in control. Then as he gets you in, he will drive you as fast and as hard as he can. I never met a drunk that meant to be one.

I have heard the saying *sipping saint*. Of course there is no such thing. They may be sipping, but they are not a saint. There is no alcohol and there are no alcoholics in heaven. If you're on the alcohol wagon, you had better get off of it now. It may seem smooth now, but it will be rocky, and its final destination is an eternal hell. Alcohol affects your reasoning. It numbs your mind and kills brain cells. How many under the influence of alcohol yield to other drugs? It works on all parts of the body. It's a deadly poison that people willingly take, just like they willingly smoke and put that poisonous nicotine into their lungs. If a person could only understand the power of a loving God to break them of their addictions. I know you don't want to hear talk about the one that controls your life. I remember I didn't like it either. But only by the grace of God did I overcome. Yes, Jesus Christ was my only way out, redeemed by the blood of Christ. But my, the scars that I carry even to this day. They were so unnecessary. You see, alcoholics are selfish. I started out just drinking on weekends, because my days off were few. Working crab lines was hard work. Years went by with me thinking I was in control, and then later in life with money in my pocket and time on my hands, lounges and bars were my meeting place. Proverbs 23:33: "Thine eyes shall behold strange women and thine heart shall utter perverse things."

It was my life, and I would live it as I wanted to. My wife didn't drink, so I went with my friends. A Miami judge stated once that 90 percent of all divorces were caused by drinking problems and that 85 percent of children in foster homes are there thanks to alcohol. Women and children by the thousands are beaten and even killed, thanks to alcohol. I was one of the 90 percent. I lost a good, faithful wife and three beautiful children. Selfish me, I walked out and left my wife and my children when they all needed me most.

Until one has the love of Christ in their heart, they don't even know what love is. Love is an action word. I don't doubt that love is the most abused word there is—the most misunderstood word. It hurts to write these things to you, but by the love of God and by his great grace, I want to help you. I am ashamed and still hurt today thinking about the nights, days, and weeks that my wife and children with broken hearts wept and cried. Mother and Dad were such strong people, but the one they loved so much was breaking their hearts. Don't get me wrong; I know that alcohol was not completely at fault. I made all the wrong choices, but anything that affects the mind is an open door for the enemy of our souls, Satan. I know that so called legal drugs prescribed by doctors are taking their toll too. And for sure, meth, crack cocaine, and heroin are killing many.

I was in Naples, Florida, some years ago to see a young man who had overdosed on drugs. I asked the doctor about the rising drug problem that was taking over and said how concerned I was about the overdosing. To my surprise, he told me that they had more people die from alcohol poison than drug overdoses. The deadliest drug, the greatest killer in our country is alcohol, and never is a word spoken against it. You ever think about it, wonder why there is a deafening silence about it? The world knows why. It's money, and most of our powerful lawmakers are alcoholics. We Christians know it's one of Satan's most powerful weapons. I have heard and read about revivals all over our great land and how bars and lounges would close down. Now I see even in our so-called Bible Belt cities, bars and lounges are on every street corner. I even remember when there was dry counties. Has God changed? Is he accepting the liquor that has taken over? Is there now darkness where once there was a great light? Are people still praying and seeking the holy God who absolutely hates sin?

Maybe we have gotten so busy we have overlooked the truth. Could it be that we have intertwined with the cares of this world so much that we have lost power with God? America needs to wake up and remember that God rained fire down upon Sodom and Gomorrah, and he will do it to America too. Friend, you can help save this country from such deserved destruction by turning to the Lord Jesus Christ for the salvation of your soul and eliminating your own personal sins that have been contributing to the sins of America. Have you ever stopped when not having a drink for several days and truly figured out the money that drinking cost you? Strange women attract you. Read Proverbs 23:23. And how much time you give to your habit that could be spent with your family? Have you ever considered the chance of causing the hurt or even death of someone, maybe a child, because of your drinking? Have you ever thought of the influence you have on your family? Have you ever considered the effect of your reputation on your children? I understand that in your excusing, selfish condition, you don't care what others think. I didn't either, being controlled by the devil. The cursing and drinking so-called friends have an influence not only in your life but on the lives of your family. It is a big word, but if you could be truthful with yourself while counting the cost of sin, which is death, you would focus on eternity. Death is on its way, and after death, the eyes open in heaven or hell.

Drinking numbs the mind and lifts God-given moral laws to invite immoral ways that can be overcome and rejected only by Jesus Christ.

I wrote this chapter on alcohol because of my close encounter with the drug that helped ruin my life. I wanted to write on three other things as well. I feel as though I have insights into these subjects from the life I have led. I may repeat things throughout this book, but some things are worth repeating.

The three subjects are: taking God out of the homes; taking God out of our schools; and taking God out of our country. Nobody has any future, any good ending, without God.

When I was a young man in grade school, I remember to this day, and I repeat this often, one of my teachers said, "The communists would take America and not fire a shot." That has stuck with me all these years. Not many things did, because I never liked school. I'm just an unlearned fisherman.

Now, as I look at our country, the big changes I can see are where they (the communists) are making a big impact. I know some will say there is a difference between socialism and communism, but I like to call them all communists. When we see this all taking place, those of us who believe God's Word know how the story ends. The Antichrist spirit is getting stronger and stronger. We are being invaded by socialists and Muslims all at one time. All Antichrists are of one voice in the dark: do away with Christians. Thank God for the Muslims who have turned to Jesus Christ our Savior. I agree with someone who said they are trying to do away with our history, our founders. Don't our lawmakers see how they have invaded our schools? (Of course they see. They are pushing the cause. Our history is Christian—all about God!

The Puritans and the Pilgrims all worshipped God. They built their towns around the most important place, the house of God. They would stray from God, and trouble would come. It would be the mercies of God to humble them before God, asking forgiveness. George Washington was one of my favorites, mainly how he was a God-fearing, praying man. When you study how he took his men through so many battles, you can't help but know it was all the hand of God. God bless America, our God-given country.

Where are we now? We elders looking back over the past fifty years all say, "What a change." As time marches on, what about the past twenty years? The past ten years? I look back thirty years ago when I was born again. In 1992, I walked out of prison a changed man through Jesus Christ. Churches had changed in a great way from what I remembered; there was compromise. People didn't believe as they once did. If you wanted to read along with the preacher from God's Holy Word, you needed a suitcase for all the different Bibles. You never knew what one he would use. I had no problem with that because I had only one Bible and still do—the King James Version.

Before I went to prison, I saw how morals had totally collapsed. The fear of God was gone. And for me to take notice with the shape I was in, it had to be bad. I can't even imagine thirty years later how bad it has truly become.

The church is as strong as the families that attend. I backslid out of a holiness church. Ran from God and later married and didn't lead my family to church. What has happened to the families of America? They have pushed God out, selling their souls for drink, drugs, and the cares of this world. Lust has become the mainstream. Books, magazines, billboards—indeed, most of all advertising—has naked or almost naked women. We've gotten so used to it that nothing seems to bother us. Most women wouldn't leave their home in their underclothing, but change the color or material, then call it a bathing suit, and out they go without a second thought. They just can't wait to see how many heads they can turn. And why not? They were raised naked from their diapers.

Children are given phones for entertainment, and through these phones, they see all that the world has to offer. By the time children are seven or eight years old, maybe even younger, they know more about sex than we older ones ever knew, and sadly, it goes beyond the teaching of God.

Is God smiling down upon our homes today? Single parents, children raising themselves. Push God out of the home, and it becomes a house of terror.

We as professing Christians have neglected the power of prayer until the God haters have closed our school doors to God. Satan has stolen our one-time morals, divided and destroyed our homes until our children know nothing about prayer. We have let these God haters take prayer out of our schools and out of our government. Take down the Ten Commandments. We stand by while these God haters confuse the minds of our children, trying to convince them they—our children—can make their own decision as to whether they want to be a boy or girl. We stand by while these God haters tell them that there is nothing wrong with a man having sexual relations with another man or a woman with a woman. They even teach them that a man can marry a man or a woman marry a woman.

There is no marriage except between a man and a woman; this is God ordained. Wake up, America. Fear God again. Leviticus 18:22 says, "Thou shalt not lie with mankind, as with womankind it is abomination."

Too many children are left on their own—left to survive in a world controlled by evil. Mothers have to let others raise them while they work, little ones whose lives are an open book. Who is filling the pages of their lives? How often are they told about Jesus Christ? If or when they make it to public school, God is not allowed there.

All of our leaders can't figure out why there is such violence in our schools. Without God, only evil exists, simple as night and day, simple as right versus wrong.

How many children are raised in houses—not homes—with alcoholics, drugs, and child molesters? How many children suffer physical and mental abuse? Children come home to an empty house.

I raised my daughter alone but was blessed with the help of my parents. But even then, we could not replace the need of a mother. The only reason she turned out as she has, a God-fearing holy lady, is because of God. She truly got that born-again experience in Jesus Christ. The things I hear and see that these elected representatives do is unbelievable. I wonder if they are that stupid or just maybe ignorant. Of course I understand that it's about self -esteem, self- power, self-advantage. But still, even their actions seem stupid. I have no education at all, but to listen to them, I feel really educated. I do know that if I wasn't a born-again child of God, I would live in fear. I sometimes wonder if they really believe in the lies or hoax about climate change, that the world is sinking or the water is rising. We already had a flood, and the rainbow from God ends that. These God haters need to know it won't be water at the next judgment but fire and brimstone.

Jesus said in John 15:18, "If the world hate you, ye know that it hated me before it hated you."

We who study God's Word know that Israel is God's chosen people. Any nation that has come against Israel has paid a price. Thank God, but by his grace we now side with Israel. When they sinned, God sent judgment. When they began to prosper and then forgot God, he sent judgment. When they repented, he was quick to forgive, to pardon. They would turn to idols, to the gods of the land, but when they returned to God, he would pardon. Is America turning God out of the great lands that he owns? How many are worshipping gods of other lands? How many of a once God-fearing land now serve idols?

Look at what an idol might be: anything or anybody that takes your time and attention more than you give to God; something or someone on which the affections are strong and often excessively set; an object of passionate devotion. I believe this could cover many things today, anything from money to jobs to hobbies to sports. What takes your time and interest? Where is your devotion?

Second Kings 24:3–4: "Surely at the commandment of the Lord came this upon Judah, to remove them out of his sight, for the sins of Manasseh, according to all that he did. And also for the innocent blood that he shed for he filled Jerusalem with innocent blood which the Lord would not pardon." The Bible says that King Manasseh filled Jerusalem with innocent blood. I wonder how it would compare with the innocent blood of babies murdered in America today. They like to say abortion rather than murder. I guess it may help them to sleep better at night, but in the eyes of God, it is murder. How can anyone professing to be a Christian vote for anyone who kills innocent babies?

Psalm 9:17: "The wicked shall be turned into hell." And all the nations that forget God. It's not the numbers of the enemy that cause our defeat; it's our commitment to God, to His Word, our obedience, our seeking His will that causes us to be overcomers and victors.

If we are faithful to God, then when the enemy comes in as a flood, God's faithfulness to his people will give us victory. Isaiah 59:19: "When the enemy shall come in like a flood, the spirit of the Lord shall lift up a standard against him." God will put him to flight. Psalm 139:14: "I will praise thee for I am fearfully and wonderfully made." Psalm 139:16: "Thine eyes did see my substance, yet being unperfect and in thy book all my members were written, which in continuance were fashioned, when as yet there was none of them."

God knows the thoughts of humans and the intentions of our hearts. All things were made by him, and therefore all things belong to him. How dare a person determine whether an innocent baby lives or dies! Psalms 22:10 "I was cast upon thee from the womb: thou art my God from my mother's belly." We the Christians of America need to wake up, speak up, and call on God! Our morals, our families, and our government need to be revived!

Psalm 13:3: "Consider and hear me, o LORD my God: lighten mine eyes, lest I sleep the sleep of death."

I'm told that we have gone from 70 percent Christians to 30 percent in our God-given land. We need to repent for our lack of concern for our country and cry to God. Stand for truth and righteousness in our own lives. Don't depart from the old paths. Hebrews 12:14: "Follow peace with all men, and holiness, without which no man shall see the Lord." We need young men and women to stand for truth along with the elders. The God haters don't mind speaking out. We hold the truth and yet are silent. Jesus Christ is our Lord and the only Savior. He is a risen Savior, alive and well. Earthly priesthood was done away with at the cross of Calvary. Jesus Christ is our high priest. We don't confess our sins to people. Buddha and Mohammed are dead. They are still in their graves. The only power they ever had was of the devil, to deceive. Another man to receive power of the devil will be the Antichrist, again to deceive and destroy until he is cast into hell. Truth will always stand, even if it has to stand alone. It will stand against the world, against family, even wives and children, even brothers and sisters.

Let me talk to the elders for a minute, for I too am an elder. How many of you elders once held the truth, but as time marched on, as pressure increased from church leaders and from children and grandchildren, you have compromised? How many of you have picked up things that you long ago laid down? How many of you are wearing things that you wouldn't have worn long ago? Things that make you look cool, things that cause you to be one of a crowd? Do you go to places that you once taught others not to go to?

How many of you dear women once allowed your God-given beauty to shine through but now hide it by applying makeup and tattoos to yourselves? How many of you once thanked God for making your natural beauty obvious to everyone but now have cluttered up that beauty by wearing jewelry and having surgery done that enhances your body?

Galatians 2:18: "For if I build again the things which I destroyed, I make myself a transgressor." I have never heard of a mother naming their little girl Jezebel—a queen from the idol-loving northern kingdom of Israel—yet they might as well because so many today are teaching them the ungodly ways of that woman.

Truth will not—indeed, cannot—compromise. When one compromises, truth leaves. It will leave a person or a church, but it will stand, because compromise and truth cannot dwell in the same temple. There is a lot of religion, but it is of the intellect, rooted in the flesh. True salvation is found in the heart, a heart that has responded to God's love, mercy, and grace.

The church is to be a light upon a hill for all the world to see, to come up to. The church does not come down to where the world is or accept the ways or the standards of the world. Morals are torn and broken. Old landmarks moved until most all boundaries are gone. People just do what is right in their own eyes. God's Word is twisted and turned to suit one's own ways. Change has come with time. I suppose it always has and always will until Jesus comes. It's all right to have change. But as change comes, God must be kept in the center.

It seems over the years that Satan's main plan is to get us so busy and distracted with things, not just ungodly things but anything to separate us from God.

The mercy of God has always reached to his creation to awaken, to shake them back to him. Is this now one of those times? Another shaking? Could it be the last shaking before he shakes heaven and earth? I fear that too many will sleep right through the shaking. They will never hear the truth crying out, "The end is near." You may say to yourselves, "What shaking? What awakening?" If you can't see and feel the darkness, the moving of the Antichrist spirit, you must be asleep. Satan knows he has but a short time. He's working hard to prepare the world for his final move.

John in the first century warns the church about the Antichrist (1 John 2:18): "Little children, it is the last time: and as ye have heard that antichrist shall come, even now are there many antichrist whereby we know that it is the last time."

Peter gives us another sign of the last days when he warns of unbelief (2 Peter 3:3 –4): "Knowing this first, that there shall come in the last days scoffers, walking after their own lists, and saying, where is the promise of his coming? For since the fathers fell asleep, all things continue as they were from the beginning of the creation."

The scoffers can't see the grace and mercy of God. Verse 9 of 2 Peter 3 tells us, "The Lord is not slack concerning his promises, as some men count slackness; but is long suffering to us ward, not willing that any should perish, but that all should come to repentance."

In my generation, we have seen the Bible attacked, Jesus attacked. In fact, every church and anybody who believes in Jesus Christ is being attacked. First John 2:22 says, "Who is a liar but he that denieth that Jesus is the Christ? He is antichrist, that denies the Father and the Son."

Satan is setting the stage for the Antichrist, tearing down homes and putting preachers in churches that are not even called of God but are only preaching for self-gratification.

Second Corinthians 11.14–15 says, "And no marvel; for Satan himself is transformed into an angel of light. Therefore it is no great thing if his ministers also be transformed as the ministers of righteousness."

A country of good morals is being destroyed, replaced with ungodliness, walking after their own lusts. God's children who are reading his Word, understanding prophecy, watch with sadness and joy—sadness for the deception but joy in knowing how the story ends. We see how Satan is setting the stage for the last scene.

"Be sober, be vigilant; because your adversary the devil, as a roaring lion, walketh about, seeking whom he may devour" (1 Peter 5:8).

I could go on and on with the signs of the end-times, but I want to bring to mind one more thing. By the Word of God, we understand that the next great event will be the calling away of the bride of Christ. We also know by God's Word that one thing had to happen before the man of sin, the Antichrist, could be revealed. "For that day shall not come (the coming of the Lord) except there come a falling away first, and that man of sin be revealed, the son of perdition" (2 Thessalonians 1:3).

God Almighty, he is God over all things. He controls all things. God the Holy Ghost is holding back the Antichrist until the appointed time. "And now ye know what withholdeth that he might be revealed in his time" (2 Thessalonians 2:6). What is this falling away? It seems to me that after some of the great revivals in the 1800s and early 1900s, things started changing. Some of the early denominations were drifting from their early beliefs. From my understanding, it was like a water faucet being turned on a little at a time until it was wide open. What do you think happened? Have you ever looked at your history to see how they lived and believed thirty, forty, and fifty years ago compared to their beliefs now? Have you ever talked to some of the elders and asked how the change took place? I'm sure there are many different answers for the falling away from what our forefathers believed. One thing for sure is God does not change. It looks to me like the change has been toward the world. I think the flesh is having its way in the fight between the flesh and the spirit. If the new ways are right, where are the old-time revivals that bring conviction, true conviction, true repentance to get our homes back together again? The love of God that makes the daddy want to get home after work and spend time with his wife and children. Where is the old-time salvation that loves the neighbor as thyself? Where is the power of the Gospel that causes the bar rooms to close because the customer quits drinking? The church can make these changes. Some will say those days are gone; there won't be any more revivals.

"Peter, standing up with the eleven, said. But this is that which was spoken by the prophet Joel: And it shall come to pass in the last days saith God, I will pour out of my Spirit upon all flesh: and your sons and your daughters shall prophesy, and your young men shall see visions, and your old men shall dream dreams. And on my servants and on my handmaidens I will pour out in those days my Spirit; and they shall prophesy" (Acts 2:16–18).

There must be a falling away. I believe we are in it. There will be an outpouring of God's spirit. It's happening in different parts of the world.

Jesus said in John 18:37, "Everyone that is of the truth heareth my voice." I think that we in America had better stop and listen. Matthew 7:14 says, "Because strait is the gate, and narrow is the way, which leadeth unto life, and few there be that find it." I myself choose the old paths, and if you could see the devil's plan and know God's mercy, you would too.

Ingram Content Group UK Ltd.
Milton Keynes UK
UKHW010935260423
420723UK00032B/189/J